Flipping the blend through MOOCs, MALL and OIL – new directions in CALL

Edited by Marina Orsini-Jones and Simon Smith

Research-publishing.net

esearch-publishing.net

Published by Research-publishing.net, a not-for-profit association
Voillans, France, info@research-publishing.net

Flipping the blend through MOOCs, MALL and OIL – new directions in CALL
Edited by Marina Orsini-Jones and Simon Smith

Disclaimer: Research-publishing.net does not take any responsibility for the content of the pages written by the authors of this book. The authors have recognised that the work described was not published before, or that it was not under consideration for publication elsewhere. While the information in this book is believed to be true and accurate on the date of its going to press, neither the editorial team nor the publisher can accept any legal responsibility for any errors or omissions. The publisher makes no warranty, expressed or implied, with respect to the material contained herein. While Research-publishing.net is committed to publishing works of integrity, the words are the authors' alone.

Trademark notice: product or corporate names may be trademarks or registered trademarks, and are used only for identification and explanation without intent to infringe.

Copyrighted material: every effort has been made by the editorial team to trace copyright holders and to obtain their permission for the use of copyrighted material in this book. In the event of errors or omissions, please notify the publisher of any corrections that will need to be incorporated in future editions of this book.

Typeset by Research-publishing.net
Cover design by © Raphaël Savina (raphael@savina.net)
Cover illustration © Marina Orsini-Jones

ISBN13: 978-2-490057-16-0 (Ebook, PDF, colour)
ISBN13: 978-2-490057-17-7 (Ebook, EPUB, colour)
ISBN13: 978-2-490057-15-3 (Paperback - Print on demand, black and white)
Print on demand technology is a high-quality, innovative and ecological printing method; with which the book is never 'out of stock' or 'out of print'.

British Library Cataloguing-in-Publication Data.
A cataloguing record for this book is available from the British Library.

Legal deposit, UK: British Library.
Legal deposit, France: Bibliothèque Nationale de France - Dépôt légal: juin 2018.

Table of contents

Notes on contributors

Editors

Marina Orsini-Jones is Associate Head of School (International) and Course Director for the MA in English Language Teaching and Applied Linguistics in the School of Humanities at Coventry University (UK). Marina is Principal Fellow and National Teaching Fellow of the Higher Education Academy and has been involved in CALL (Computer Assisted Language Learning) since 1986. She obtained her doctorate in 2012 with a dissertation titled: *Towards a role-reversal model of action-research-supported threshold concepts pedagogy in languages and linguistics.* She has contributed to over 100 national and international conferences (including as invited plenary speaker) and has published work on CALL, research-led curricular innovation, threshold concepts in languages and linguistics, MOOCs, telecollaboration, and digital literacies. She has been awarded numerous pedagogical grants. Her most recent publication, with Fiona Lee, is: *Intercultural Communicative Competence for Global Citizenship: Identifying Rules of Engagement in Telecollaboration* (2018).

Simon Smith is Senior Lecturer in Academic English and Course Director for English for International Business in the School of Humanities at Coventry University. He has published on data-driven learning and the use of corpora in Chinese and English language teaching, and co-edited, with Dr Bin Zou and Prof. Michael Hoey, a book on *Corpus Linguistics in Chinese Contexts* (2015). He teaches English for Academic Purposes and English for Specific Purposes at both undergraduate and postgraduate level, and Chinese to undergraduates. He contributes to the research methods, genre analysis, and corpus linguistics modules on the MA in English Language Teaching and Applied Linguistics. He is involved in Online International Learning projects with overseas partners and is researching the CMC features of OIL exchanges. He is Research Associate in Coventry's Centre for Global Learning: Education and Attainment (GLEA), and a member of the research group Corpus Linguistics at Coventry (CLaC).

Authors

Marwa Alnajjar is a tutor in English Language at the Royal College of Surgeons in the Ireland-Medical University of Bahrain, and is presently teaching English for nursing in addition to an IELTS preparatory course. Previously, she taught English as a foreign language at elementary schools in the public sector in the Kingdom of Bahrain. She was awarded her Master of Arts in English Language Teaching with Distinction from Coventry University, United Kingdom, in 2016. She was part of the first cohort to graduate from Bahrain Teacher's College, University of Bahrain, with a Bachelor of Education. She was awarded the Dean's Award for Academic Excellence and included in the President's List of Honours. Her current research interests include teacher training, vocabulary teaching and learning, materials design, and utilising computer-assisted language learning tools in the English language classroom.

Stephen Bax: please refer to the dedication for Stephen's biographical information.

Kate Borthwick is Principal Enterprise Fellow (Technology Enhanced Learning) in Modern Languages and Linguistics and Director of Curriculum Innovation in the Faculty of Humanities and Director of Programme Development (online learning) in the University's Digital Learning team at the University of Southampton (UK). She is a linguist who spent ten years teaching English to international students across the globe and in universities around the UK, before taking a Masters at Newcastle University in the use of technology in language teaching. She oversees two repositories of OERs: LanguageBox and HumBox. She is the course designer for 4 FutureLearn/ UoS MOOCs: 'Understanding Language: learning and teaching', 'Agincourt 1415: myth and reality', 'English Medium Instruction for Academics', and 'Jane Austen: myth, reality, and global celebrity.' She has been invited to speak at national and international conferences. She was conference chair for the annual EuroCALL conference in 2017. Kate received a Vice-Chancellor's Award (individual) for internationalisation in 2016, for her work on the MOOC 'Understanding Language'.

Billy Brick is Languages Centre Manager and Principal Lecturer in the School of Humanities at Coventry University. He is also Senior Fellow of the Higher Education Academy and a member of the Chartered Institute of Linguists. He teaches German language, Materials and Syllabus Design in a Multimedia World to undergraduate students, and Computer Assisted Language Learning at Masters level, and has been involved with numerous JISC/HEA projects including Coventry Online Writing Lab (COWL) and Humbox, an OER project for the humanities. He has published numerous articles in the field of technology and language learning and regularly contributes papers to conferences. His current research focus is in social media and language learning, and he is currently leading a project to evaluate the effectiveness of Duolingo in beginners' language classes.

Abraham Cerveró-Carrascosa is the Erasmus coordinator in the Education Unit at Florida Universitària in València, Spain, where he also lectures in TEFL (Teaching English as a Foreign Language) in English and Catalan. He is moreover an examiner for the official B2 English and CLIL methodology tests. He has lectured at the Faculty of Education in the University of València, where he is in the process of completing his PhD dissertation on the role of metacognition in the writing processes of pre-service primary teachers. Abraham has contributed to numerous national and international conferences and published work on TEFL and multilingual policies in primary, secondary, and higher education.

Courtney Green is an undergraduate student on the English and TEFL course at Coventry University. She managed the FloCo project from Spain while on her TEFL Erasmus placement in the Education Unit at Florida Universitària in València in academic year 2017-2018, working in collaboration with Elwyn Lloyd and Abraham Cerveró-Carrascosa.

Yan Jiao is Headmaster of an independent school as well as a teacher educator at Harbin International Centre for Cultural Exchanges, which is a subsidiary of the Wei Di Nai De Translation & Interpreting Company located in Shanghai, China. He received a Master's Degree in English Language Teaching (ELT) and Applied Linguistics at Coventry University in the UK. He is currently planning to establish an online English Language Learning App aiming to support the development of learner autonomy in ELT. He can be contacted at jiaoy6@uni. coventry.ac.uk or jiaoy6@icloud.com.

Nicole Keng is Lecturer in English at the University of Vaasa, Finland. She holds an MA in TESOL (Teaching English to Speakers of Other Languages) from Christ Church University, and a PhD in Language Teaching and Learning from the University of York (UK). Keng has extensive experience of teaching English for Academic Purposes to students of all levels in China and the UK. Her research interests include corpora in language learning, cross-cultural communication, CALL, and digitalisation in language teaching and learning. Her teaching in Finland involves English courses at both undergraduate and postgraduate level, and she creates and develops courses combining language, communication, and employability skills. Her recent research interests mainly involve embedding action research in teaching and learning and Online International Learning projects with partners from different countries to develop internationalisation and digitalisation at universities in Finland.

Agnes Kukulska-Hulme is Professor of Learning Technology and Communication in the Institute of Educational Technology at The Open University, and Past-President of the International Association for Mobile Learning. Her recent projects include the EU-funded MASELTOV project on personalised technologies for social inclusion, the British Council project on Mobile Pedagogy for English Language Teaching, and the MK: Smart SALSA project on language learning in the next generation of smart cities. Among her publications is the co-edited book, *Mobile Learning: The Next Generation published* (2016). She supervises doctoral students researching mobile and social learning, professional development, and knowledge sharing.

Elwyn Lloyd is Course Director for TEFL (Teaching English as a Foreign Language) in the School of Humanities at Coventry University (UK). Previous to his current role he had accumulated extensive experience as an English teacher and Director of Studies at language schools in Spain, and he obtained his MA in Language Learning and Technology from the University of Hull. Elwyn's research interests are centred on the application of telecollaboration, social networking sites, and mobile technology in language learning and teaching. His most recent publications and conference presentations relate to the use of Web 2.0 tools for language learning and teaching. Elwyn also coordinates the delivery of the Cambridge CELTA (Certificate in English Language Teaching to Adults) at Coventry University.

An Ostyn is an experienced lecturer in Corporate Communications and Business English at VIVES University of Applied Sciences (Kortrijk, Belgium). She is the editor of a research newsletter at VIVES and a regular presenter at VIVES and international events, seminars and conferences. Being involved in internationalisation of higher education at VIVES, she has been a guest lecturer at European and transatlantic universities. She is also the co-organiser of a collaborative online international learning project for Business English students. In addition, she coaches communication skills to event management students.

Minh Tuan Phi is an Academic Coordinator and English teacher at Institution of American Education in Hanoi, Vietnam. During his undergraduate studies majoring in International Economics, he worked as a private tutor which fuelled his desire to become an English teacher. In 2013, he became an English assistant lecturer at Hanoi Open University, where he taught General English and Academic English. This job provided him motivation to further his study at Coventry University, where he received his Master of Arts in English Language Teaching and Applied Linguistics with distinction in 2017. During the time at Coventry University, he gave several talks on his learning journey and took part in the ELTRA (English Language Teaching and Applied Linguistics) BMELTT (Blending MOOCs into English Language Teacher Training) project with staff and students from the Netherlands, China, and the UK. His research interests include autonomy, teacher education, and educational technology.

Andrew Preshous is Senior Lecturer in Academic English in the School of Humanities at Coventry University and specialises in EAP, teacher training, and Business English. He has taught English in a variety of contexts in Greece, Poland, Hong Kong, Malaysia, and the UK. This experience includes developing and delivering specialist ESP courses such as English Pronunciation for Malaysian newsreaders and English for the Hotel Industry. Andrew's current areas of interest include subject specific materials design, creating screencasts to provide feedback, and online international learning projects. He is a CELTA approved teacher trainer and is also interested in teacher development. He has published a number of articles relating to EAP, Business English and OIL, and an IELTS coursebook (*IELTS Foundation*, 2004).

Simon Smith: please refer to the editor's section for Simon's biographical information.

Reviewers

Kate Borthwick: please refer to the author's section for Kate's biographical information.

Mike Cribb is Senior Lecturer in linguistics in the School of Humanities at Coventry University and specialises in discourse analysis, first and second language acquisition, semantics, and phonology. He has published work and presented papers in these areas of interest. He also takes an interest in intercultural communication issues and MOOCs. He has worked overseas, teaching English language and linguistics in the Far East.

David Jones is now retired and was formerly Head of the Department of English and Languages at Coventry University. He has published on CALL and on threshold concepts pedagogy.

Kan Qian is Senior Lecturer in the School of Languages and Applied Linguistics, The Open University (UK). She has a PhD in Linguistics from Lancaster University, and is Senior Fellow of the British Higher Education Academy. Her research focuses on the use of technologies for the learning and teaching of languages: interactions in online discussion forums, mobile language learning, and mobile application design, eTandem learning, and language MOOC design.

Fiona Lee is Lecturer in French and Academic Skills in the School of Humanities at Coventry University. She has recently obtained her MA in English Language Teaching with distinction. She has published work on reflective practice and action-research-informed curricular design. She is Associate Fellow of the Higher Education Academy.

Acknowledgements

We would like to thank all the staff and students who have participated in the projects reported in this collection. We would also like to thank the British Council for the award of the English Language Teaching Research Award that partially funded the symposium where the papers were presented and Dr Frank Magee, Head of the School of Humanities, who also provided financial support for it. A big thank you also goes to our partners who participated in the symposium and its round table on the 30th of June, in particular the staff and students from the Hogeschool Utrecht, for their useful insights on how they utilised the MOOC, and Dr Bin Zou from Xi'an Jiaotong-Liverpool University for the background information on MOOCs in China. We would also like to give our thanks to the (then) staff from the Disruptive Media Learning Laboratory at Coventry University, Prof. Sylvester Arnab and Sarah Kernaghan-Andrews in particular, who provided academic and technical support respectively for the event.

Also, it would not have been possible to organise the symposium without the help received from the admin team, Mrs Sue Grant and Ms Caroline Parkinson and the volunteer student helpers from the MA in English Language Teaching and Applied Linguistics.

A big thank you goes to Stephen Bax's family for giving us permission to write up his contribution as a paper for this collection and to Andrew Bax, Stephen's son, and Qian Kan (OU), for reviewing it.

A final thank you goes to Sylvie Thouësny, whose efficiency and patience made this publication possible.

Marina Orsini-Jones and Simon Smith

Dedication

Marina Orsini-Jones[1] and Simon Smith[2]

Like the IJCALLT (International Journal of Computer Assisted Language Learning and Teaching) special issue based on the BMELTT (Blending MOOCs in English Teacher Training) Symposium published in December 2017[3] (Orsini-Jones, 2017), this conference proceedings collection is dedicated to the memory of Professor Stephen Bax, who died on the 22nd of November 2017. Stephen was professor of Modern Languages and Linguistics at the Open University.

Stephen was a plenary speaker at the BMELTT Symposium, held in June 2017 at Coventry University. His speech was entitled 'MOOCs as a new technology: approaches to normalising the MOOC experience for our learners' and it has been reconstructed from the video-recording here with the support and help of his son, Andy, his family, Professor Qian Kan, one of his close collaborators from the Open University, and his MA alumna Nicole Keng, whom we would like to warmly thank for giving us permission to do so.

Stephen started his teaching career as an English tutor in Sudan and the Middle East, and was one of the early pioneers of English teaching with the British Council in that part of the world. He drew on his own rich experience of teaching English as a foreign language, as well as his personal commitment to language learning, to inspire and motivate many people – both learners and teachers of language.

1. Coventry University, Coventry, United Kingdom; lsx008@coventry.ac.uk

2. Coventry University, Coventry, United Kingdom; ab3336@coventry.ac.uk

3. Republished with kind permissions from IGI Global. We would like to thank the editorial board at IJCALLT, in particular Dr Bin Zou, Editor in Chief, the Director of Intellectual Property and Contacts, and Mrs Colleen Moore, Editorial Assistant, for giving us permission to reproduce parts of the dedication to Stephen Bax contained in the Special issue edited by Orsini-Jones (Volume 4, 2017).

How to cite: Orsini-Jones, M., & Smith, S. (2018). Dedication. In M. Orsini-Jones & S. Smith (Eds), *Flipping the blend through MOOCs, MALL and OIL – new directions in CALL* (pp. xiii-xiv). Research-publishing.net. https://doi.org/10.14705/rpnet.2018.23.782

His interest in and talent for technology led him to start drawing on digital resources in his teaching practice. He was also an early and important contributor to research in this field. His seminal article 'CALL, past, present and future', published in System in 2003 was awarded the Elsevier prize. Stephen received the International Distinguished Researcher Award in 2014 from the International TESOL Foundation for his expertise in language learning and testing.

His interest in texts and technology motivated him to develop the tool textinspector.com, leading this year, 2017, to his ELTon award for digital innovation in English teaching and testing. His recent work decoding the 15th century Voynich manuscript shows the fascinating diversity of Stephen's research interests, as well as his enthusiasm for innovative and challenging scholarship. Never a lone researcher, he thrived on sharing ideas with colleagues and students, inspiring others to conduct ground-breaking research in our field.

Stephen was a model teacher, who kept his finger on the pulse of new developments in the industry, ready to take on board new knowledge and skills – and he encouraged everyone else to do the same. As a teacher, he always made time for students. He was always encouraging and supportive, and constantly showed his faith in his students, giving them the confidence to set and meet challenging targets. He was also a very inspirational teacher trainer.

We were very honoured to be able to invite him as a speaker to share his insights into MOOCs and the digital learning world. We are deeply saddened by his passing, only a few short months after he joined us at BMELTT. He will be sorely missed by many readers of this collection, as well as those involved in producing it.

References

Orsini-Jones, M. (Ed.). (2017). Dedication. *International Journal of Computer-Assisted Language Learning and Teaching (IJCALLT)*, *7*(4), vi.

Preface

Marina Orsini-Jones[1] and Simon Smith[2]

This special issue collection derives from an international symposium held at Coventry University (CU) on the 29th and 30th of June 2017: *BMELTT (Blending MOOCs for English Language Teacher Training) – the Symposium: Flipping the Blend through MALL (Mobile Assisted Language Learning), MOOCs (Massive Open Online Courses) and BOIL (Blended Online Intercultural Learning) – New Directions in CALL (Computer Assisted Language Learning)*[3]. The symposium was jointly funded by an English Language Teaching Research Award (ELTRA) by the British Council, by Coventry University (School of Humanities, Faculty of Arts and Humanities) and by staff based in the Disruptive Media Learning Laboratory (DMLL), based in the Lanchester Library at Coventry University. The symposium attracted around 100 participants from over ten countries around the world and provided a snapshot of how CALL is evolving in the 21st century. The somewhat provocative title aimed at stimulating a discussion on how new technologies are supporting the development of fluid blended learning models, where existing technologies are re-purposed for the pedagogical needs and wants of their users.

The conceptualisation of 'blended learning' has evolved considerably since it was explored by Bonk and Graham in 2006. MOOCs, MALL, and Online Intercultural/International Learning (OIL) have provided innovative opportunities for 'distributed flip' models (Sandeen, 2013), where learners in distant locations can engage in blended social-collaboration in multiple modes, blending face-to-face activities in classroom settings with discussions on institutional Virtual Learning Environments (VLE) (like Moodle, BlackBoard,

1. Coventry University, Coventry, United Kingdom; lsx008@coventry.ac.uk

2. Coventry University, Coventry, United Kingdom; ab3336@coventry.ac.uk

3. https://youtu.be/tUJqvbg_q1M

How to cite this chapter: Orsini-Jones, M., & Smith, S. (2018). Preface. In M. Orsini-Jones & S. Smith (Eds), *Flipping the blend through MOOCs, MALL and OIL – new directions in CALL* (pp. xv-xxii). Research-publishing.net. https://doi.org/10.14705/rpnet.2018.23.783

and Canvas), enhanced by global interactions on Open Educational Resource (OER) platforms, such as MOOCs (e.g. *FutureLearn*[4] and *Coursera*). The affordances of Web 2.0 technologies can blur the lines between face-to-face and blended modes of delivery, between formal and informal learning, and between teachers and learners.

The discussion with the participants who took part in the round table at the BMELTT symposium, which included one of the partners from China and all the partners from the Netherlands who had taken part in the ELTRA project – see Orsini-Jones, Conde Gafaro, and Altamimi (2017) (including some students), illustrated moreover that many of the terms used in CALL are often interpreted in different ways and given different teaching and learning contexts. For example, the conceptualisation of 'MOOC' would appear to be closer to an OER in the UK, while it seems to be closer to an institutional VLE in China.

The symposium also highlighted the need to review how we interpret communicative competence in CALL/MALL Web 2.0 settings (see Orsini-Jones & Lee, 2018 on this point). An interesting feature of the symposium contributions were the talks by 'expert students', such as Minh Tuan Phi and Yan Jiao, who carried out blended MOOC curricular evaluations and research based on studies previously conducted by their tutors. This provided an interesting role-reversal perspective on blended-MOOC flips.

The first chapter of this collection is based on the keynote by **Agnes Kukulska-Hulme** on day one of the BMELTT symposium (29th of June): *Mobile assistance for personal learning on a massive scale*. Kukulska-Hulme, based at the Open University, reports on an interesting project she is carrying out where a MALL App has been designed to support the English language needs of refugees in a contextual way, guiding them through the services they need to access. This project provides an excellent example of the kind of research-informed "ethical CALL" (or MALL) that can be produced with the support of new technologies.

---

4. https://www.futurelearn.com/courses/understanding-language

The second chapter, *MOOCs as a new technology: approaches to normalising the MOOC experience for our learners*, is the plenary from the second day of the symposium (30th of June) by **Stephen Bax** (Open University), when Stephen entertained us with pictures of very odd technology that never became normalised, e.g. 'The Isolator' (see the presentation available at the link in the references to this section, Bax, 2017). In chapter two, Bax discusses MOOC 'normalisation', using as starting points his seminal papers *CALL, Past, Present and Future* (Bax, 2003), *Normalisation revisited: the effective use of technology in language education* (Bax, 2011), and his most recent book on MOOCs with Kan (Kan & Bax, 2017). He outlines the current landscape with regard to language learning MOOCs, drawing on successful Open University projects in Spanish and Italian. It looks critically at where language MOOCs seem to be potentially most valuable, and also at aspects of the experience which seem to have impeded normalisation.

In chapter three, *What our MOOC did next: embedding, exploiting, and extending an existing MOOC to fit strategic purposes and priorities*, **Kate Borthwick**, Director of Programme Development (online and blended learning) at the University of Southampton, reports on the evolution of the creation, evaluation, and continuous re-design of the MOOC *Understanding Language: Learning and Teaching*[5], which she has managed in collaboration with the British Council for seven runs to date (at the time of writing, May 2018). She concludes by discussing how a MOOC can support the key priorities of a Higher Education institution, marketing included.

In chapters four and five, 'expert students' discuss the advantages and disadvantages of integrating MOOCs into the curriculum of the Master of Arts (MA) in English Language Teaching and Applied Linguistics at Coventry University. The two chapters align with previous related literature on the role-reversal thresholds concept pedagogy model (Orsini-Jones, 2014), where 'expert students' engage with research topics that have been explored by their tutors and,

---

5. https://www.futurelearn.com/courses/understanding-language

in doing so, help them (the tutors) to see their practice and research through the students' eyes (as also discussed in Orsini-Jones et al., 2017).

In chapter four, *Integrating a MOOC into the MA curriculum: an 'expert' student's reflections on blended learning*, **Minh Tuan Phi**, MA in ELTAL alumnus, currently Academic Coordinator, IvyPrep Education in Hanoi, Vietnam, presents a student-centred view of the integration of the MOOC discussed by Borthwick into the curriculum of the MA in English Language Teaching and Applied Linguistics at Coventry University. The sudy reports on how he decided to replicate related studies carried out by Orsini-Jones (2015) for his MA dissertation and explores how a blended MOOC approach impacted on his beliefs and his identity as an autonomous teacher of English, which he had also explored in a previous related publication (Phi, 2017).

In *Understanding learner autonomy through MOOC-supported blended learning environments: an investigation into Chinese MA ELT students' beliefs* – chapter five – **Yan Jiao**, another alumnus of the MA in ELTAL and currently employed as teacher trainer at Harbin International Centre for Cultural Exchanges in China, also links to the theme of MOOCs and their integration into the formal curriculum. Like Phi's, this work is based on the author's MA dissertation, but it discusses a different MOOC: *Exploring the world of English language teaching* (Jiao, 2018). Also like Phi, Jiao explores the troublesome nature of autonomy in language learning for his Chinese peers and discusses how the MOOC integration can support them with understanding this concept. His interesting findings illustrate how experienced Chinese teachers on the MA programme appear to pay 'lip service' to the adoption of autonomy in theory, but do not apply it in practice when engaging in micro-teaching, while less experienced teachers on the MA in ELTAL are more willing to embrace pedagogies that are alien to their Confucian teacher-centred contexts/background.

This collection also contains two chapters that relate to OIL, also called Online Intercultural Exchange (OIE), Collaborative Online International Learning (COIL), telecollaboration (see Orsini-Jones & Lee, 2018, on this), or Virtual Exchange (VE) in the Erasmus+ literature. The title of the symposium referred to BOIL, which was a bit 'tongue in cheek' and was meant to highlight the face-to-face side that is normally inherent in OIL projects, but which gets lost in the 'O' for online. In the first study – chapter six – *OIL for English for business: the intercultural product pitch,* **Andrew Preshous**, Senior Lecturer in Academic English at Coventry University, **An Ostyn**, Business English Lecturer at VIVES University College (Kortrijk, Belgium), and **Nicole Keng**, Lecturer in English at the University of Vaasa, Finland, report on how OIL helps to integrate soft skills into the academic curriculum, as well as providing students with international interaction opportunities and develop intercultural awareness. In this project, Malaysian, Chinese, and Indonesian International Business students in the UK established links with their Belgian or Finnish peers online using a tailor-made Moodle platform, then delivered a product pitch presentation before responding to another group's output. Students' feedback on the project was very positive and the tutors were also pleased with the level of digital literacies practised by students.

The second piece of work on OIL, *A role-reversal model of telecollaborative practice: the student-driven and student-managed FloCo (Florida Universitària/Coventry University)* – chapter seven – is by **Elwyn Lloyd**, Senior Lecturer in TEFL (Teaching English as a Foreign Language), **Abraham Cerveró-Carrascosa**, Lecturer in English Language Teaching at the Unitat d'Educació, Florida Universitària in València, Spain, and **Courtney Green,** a Coventry English and TEFL third year undergraduate student currently on her placement abroad at the Florida Universitària to teach English. This chapter reports on *FloCo*, a telecollaborative project where, like in the research reported by Phi and Jiao, the roles of teacher and student were reversed. Green had taken part in the online intercultural exchange *MexCo* (Mexico/Coventry), between Coventry and Mexico (Orsini-Jones et al., 2017), in her first year at university and decided to set up a similar exchange between the class of students she was teaching in Spain and Year 1 students on Spanish degrees at CU in collaboration with Lloyd and Cerveró-Carrascosa. The shared 'expert student' staff reflections on the project are reported in this chapter and compared with the outcomes of related online intercultural exchanges (e.g. *MexCo* and *CoCo: Coventry/Colmar*).

In *Chinese segmentation and collocation: a platform for blended learning* – chapter eight – **Simon Smith**, Senior Lecturer in Academic English and Course Director for English for Business, discusses an innovative approach to teaching Mandarin through blended learning with a corpus-based platform. Smith argues that very little research has been carried out on inductive or autonomous learning in the realm of collocation acquisition. He proposes a new Chinese implementation of a trusted corpus-based platform, currently available for English learning, accompanied and enhanced by a data-driven approach to Chinese segmentation, whereby different ways of carving up a given sentence are selectively displayed to the learner.

In the final study in this collection – chapter nine –, *Student-teachers' beliefs concerning the usability of digital flashcards in ELT*, **Marwa Alnajjar** and **Billy Brick** report on an interesting qualitative study on the beliefs of student-teachers on the MA in English language teaching at Coventry University regarding the usability of three digital flashcard websites to teach English language. The study reports that despite their positive feedback on this new technology, participants appeared reluctant to adopt it because they did not feel comfortable with teaching it to their students. This discrepancy between teachers' beliefs and teachers' practice, which also emerged from Jiao's study in this collection, appears to be a recurrent theme in language teacher education. It is hoped that collections of practice-oriented papers on CALL like this one can dispel language teachers' fear of technology, go beyond the 'wow' factor, and support the normalisation of useful new CALL platforms.

We hope that the readers enjoy the variety of OIL, MALL, MOOC, and other e-learning assisted language learning studies reported here. We would like to thank all the contributors and a very heartfelt thank you also goes to the reviewers who volunteered to support the editing of this collection, namely: Kate Borthwick, Mike Cribb, David Jones, and Fiona Lee. A very special thank you goes to Qian Kan and Andrew Bax for helping with the writing up of Stephen's chapter and to Andrew Bax and family for granting us permission to write up the chapter from the video-recording.

References

Bax, S. (2003). CALL – past, present and future. *System, 31*(1), 13-28. https://doi.org/10.1016/S0346-251X(02)00071-4

Bax, S. (2011). Normalisation revisited: the effective use of technology in language education. *IJCALLT, 1*(2), 1-15. https://doi.org/10.4018/ijcallt.2011040101

Bax, S. (2017). *MOOCs as a new technology: approaches to normalising the MOOCs experience for our learners.* Paper presented at the B-MELTT: Flipping the Blend through MALL, MOOCs and BOIL – New Directions in CALL Symposium, Coventry, UK: Coventry University. https://youtu.be/S1ZJf74HxnA

Bonk, C. J., & Graham, C. A. (2006). *The handbook of blended learning: global perspectives, local designs.* Pfeiffer/Wiley.

Jiao, Y. (2018). *Understanding learner autonomy through MOOC-supported blended learning environment: an investigation into Chinese MAELT students' beliefs.* MA dissertation submitted at Coventry University, Coventry, for the award of an MA in English Language Teaching and Applied Linguistics.

Kan, Q., & Bax, S. (Eds). (2017). *Beyond the language classroom: researching MOOCs and other innovations.* Research-publishing.net. https://doi.org/10.14705/rpnet.2017.mooc2016.9781908416537

Orsini-Jones, M. (2014). Towards a role-reversal model of threshold concept pedagogy. In C. O'Mahony, A. Buchanan, M. O'Rourke & B. Higgs (Eds), *Threshold concepts: from personal practice to communities of practice.* Proceedings of the National Academy's Sixth Annual Conference and the Fourth Biennial Threshold Concepts Conference [e-publication], January 2014, NAIRTL. http://www.nairtl.ie/documents/EPub_2012Proceedings.pdf#page=88

Orsini-Jones, M. (2015). Integrating a MOOC into the MA in English language teaching at Coventry University: innovation in blended learning practice. *Higher Education Academy.* https://www.heacademy.ac.uk/sites/default/files/marina_orsini_jones_final_1.pdf

Orsini-Jones, M., Conde Gafaro, B., & Altamimi, S. (2017). Integrating a MOOC into the postgraduate ELT curriculum: reflecting on students' beliefs with a MOOC blend. In Q. Kan & S. Bax (Eds), *Beyond the language classroom: researching MOOCs and other innovations* (pp. 71-83). Research-publishing.net. https://doi.org/10.14705/rpnet.2017.mooc2016.672

Orsini-Jones, M., & Lee, F. (2018). *Intercultural communicative competence for global citizenship: identifying rules of engagement in telecollaboration.* Palgrave MacMillan. https://doi.org/10.1057/978-1-137-58103-7

Orsini-Jones, M., Lloyd, E., Cribb, M., Lee, F., Bescond, G., Ennagadi, A., & García, B. (2017). Embedding an online intercultural learning project into the curriculum: the trouble with cyberpragmatics. *International Journal of Computer-Assisted Language Learning and Teaching (IJCALLT), 7*(1), 50-65. https://doi.org/10.4018/IJCALLT.2017010104

Phi, M. T. (2017). Becoming autonomous learners to become autonomous teachers: investigation on a MOOC blend. *International Journal of Computer-Assisted Language Learning and Teaching, 7*(4) 13-32. https://doi.org/10.4018/IJCALLT.2017100102

Sandeen, C. (2013). Integrating MOOCs into traditional higher education: the emerging "MOOC 3.0" era. *Change, 45*(6), 34-39. https://doi.org/10.1080/00091383.2013.842103

1 Mobile assistance for personal learning on a massive scale

Agnes Kukulska-Hulme[1]

Abstract

Despite efforts to increase participation in education across the globe, it remains an inaccessible right for millions of children and adults. Mobile learning, and specifically 'mobile assistance', can provide personal support to learners when teachers are scarce or learners have pressing individual goals. MASELTOV was a project which implemented mobile assistance for migrants, comprising a suite of smartphone tools and services for orientation in a new environment and everyday language learning. Experiences gained from this project invite reflection on what are the unique qualities of teachers and human assistance. As we enter a new era of pervasive applications of artificial intelligence (AI), there are concerns that AI will encroach on the territory of the teacher. However, it is possible that intelligent assistants can be designed and used in such a way that they complement and enhance what human teachers are uniquely able to do. It is important to ask how less developed societies will be included in these advancements. The answer can emerge from greater clarity around the nature and capabilities of mobile and intelligent assistance.

Keywords: mobile learning, intelligent assistants, teacher competences, mass education challenges.

1. The Open University, Milton Keynes, United Kingdom; agnes.kukulska-hulme@open.ac.uk

How to cite this chapter: Kukulska-Hulme, A. (2018). Mobile assistance for personal learning on a massive scale. In M. Orsini-Jones & S. Smith (Eds), *Flipping the blend through MOOCs, MALL and OIL – new directions in CALL* (pp. 1-7). Research-publishing.net. https://doi.org/10.14705/rpnet.2018.23.784

1. Introduction

In the first two decades of the 21st century, there have been significant efforts to increase participation in education at all levels across the globe and to improve the quality of provision (UNESCO, 2015; UN, 2017). Yet education remains an inaccessible right for millions of children and adults. It is estimated that across the world, more than 72 million children of primary education age are not in school and 759 million adults are illiterate (Humanium, 2017). Furthermore, growing numbers of displaced children and adults have very limited access to learning. Refugee children are five times more likely to be out of school than non-refugee children, and just one percent of refugees attend university (UNHCR, 2016). Addressing the lack of education opportunities for women and girls is another major challenge highlighted by the World Bank (2017) and UNESCO (2017a). Efforts to provide education and support continue to be hampered by a chronic shortage of high quality learning materials and suitably qualified teachers (UNESCO, 2017b).

Technological innovation can help solve some of these problems. Efforts to widen access have in recent years included technology-supported approaches, such as massive open online courses (MOOCs) and growing collections of open educational resources (Scanlon, McAndrew, & O'Shea, 2015). Mobile learning has also been recognised as a valuable approach to widening access, including for the education and professional development of teachers (UNESCO, 2017b). Furthermore, technological advances create opportunities to match educational provision more closely to individuals' needs, to track their progress and support them in adaptive ways (Dziuban, Moskal, Johnson, & Evans, 2017) on their computers, tablets, or smartphones.

As we enter a new era of more pervasive applications of AI (Boden, 2016), there are concerns around AI replacing jobs and encroaching on the territory of the teacher (Von Radowitz, 2017). However, it is possible that at least one form of AI, namely intelligent assistants, can be used in such a way that they complement and perhaps enhance what human teachers are uniquely able to do. Intelligent (or 'smart') assistants are already encountered on smartphones, wearables such as watches and glasses, and smart home devices, and they are starting to appear in humanoid form as social robots (Li, Kizilcec, Bailenson, & Ju, 2016). As advanced societies begin to adopt a growing array of intelligent assistants, it is important to ask how less economically advantaged learners and less developed societies will be included. The answer may partly emerge from greater clarity around the nature and capabilities of mobile and intelligent assistance.

2. Learning from experiences of mobile assistance for migrants

Our approach at The Open University has been to conceptualise increasingly smart forms of mobile assistance on the basis of what we have discovered through a series of research projects on learning with smartphones, where the focus has been on opening up learning opportunities to migrants and refugees. These projects have focused on informal, everyday language learning within a broader range of daily experiences and challenges. The premise is that people who experience involuntary displacement, as well as those who are mobile by choice, can be in a position to derive benefit from flexible and mobile learning afforded by smartphones and other portable devices, but they will need support. This work has highlighted the issue of mediation and facilitation of learning: teachers are not always available when people want to learn a little every day, or if they wish to work on a particular skill or a pressing personal goal – so who can help them? It might be other people, other learners, or diverse forms of assistance provided or mediated by technology.

The Open University was a partner in the MASELTOV project (www.maseltov. eu; Kukulska-Hulme et al., 2015) in which the project consortium developed a 'mobile assistant' in the form of a prototype suite of context-aware and integrated services and tools for recent immigrants in Europe that they could access via a single app on a smartphone. These learners from other continents appreciated the opportunity to engage in daily language practice and have access to various forms of assistance and support. The prototype services and tools included help with moving around a city, language lessons, a translation tool, a game for playful cultural learning, healthcare information, recommendations (what to do or where to go, based on interests and movements), an online social forum, and a social radar to summon volunteers willing to help. Learners could also track their own progress in some respects, for example their completion of language lessons and which tools they had used. They could learn individually or in groups (with friends or family). As previously stated in Kukulska-Hulme (2016), the research touched on the issue of how new configurations of human assistance – combinations of teachers, friends, volunteers, mentors, and online communities – together with the tools provided on the smartphone, could support mobile learners in their efforts to make use of learning opportunities in their daily lives.

The learners needed considerable help to understand and engage with this new way of learning. It was important for them to have social contact, which could take place in workshops, via the app, or through ongoing interactions with a facilitator and a researcher. This enabled cognitive and social support; the learners could share experiences of using the app, ask questions about language and culture, and help others. Often working in groups with others who had the same first language, they could switch between languages when they needed or chose to do so. Learner feedback and observations in workshops suggested that the human contact was instrumental in motivating the learners, sustaining their engagement, and encouraging them to develop new learning habits (for further discussion of mobile assistance, see also Kukulska-Hulme, 2016). Further research would be needed to establish more precisely the value and functions of human and non-human assistance and support, in the contexts of both informal and formal learning, and specifically in relation to language learning.

3.   Intelligent assistance – the next generation

What are the unique qualities of language teachers in a world where life and learning are increasingly suffused with technology? Philp (2017) offers one perspective: "language learning involves much more than grammatical or lexical knowledge: it involves developing the competence to communicate in ways that are appropriate to the 'who, what, when, where and why' of communication… the teacher plays a vital role in encouraging learners, in providing sufficient support during challenging tasks so that learners are pushed, yet successful" (p.17). Philp notes that outside of formal lessons, learners might undertake autonomous work and teachers can support these practices "by modelling strategies for coping with unfamiliar input, for negotiating problems in output and by providing feedback that highlights problem areas and encourages self-correction or further exploration by the learner" (p.17).

It seems that human capabilities are far in advance of AI, yet in the near future mobile and intelligent assistance is set to increase and diversify. Mobile assistance can be as simple as a translation facility on a mobile phone; but intelligent agents and assistants that currently answer questions and give recommendations on smartphones are likely to evolve into more sophisticated human-like help and will challenge human-led teaching and training (see for example Macedonia, Groher, & Roithmayr, 2014). Next generation voice-controlled personal assistants will be able to perform thousands of tasks and will be integrated into everyday objects and companion robots (Kim, Kim, Jun, & Kim, 2017). People will increasingly use voice communication with devices which may or may not 'speak' a familiar language, thereby adding complexity to language teaching and learning. Until recently, this seemed like a distant prospect but in technologically advanced societies that is no longer the case.

4.   Conclusions

Mobile assistance is an important concept that needs further exploration in the face of growing demand for educational opportunities across the globe. The MASELTOV approach was scalable in terms of giving large numbers of people access to an app. A highly personal learning approach could be adopted by the app users, especially if they were prepared to think about their own learning goals and needs and were not afraid to try out a range of unfamiliar tools and services. Human involvement and assistance seemed to play an important role in encouraging and supporting the learners, although no teachers were directly involved. Emerging intelligent assistants can be seen as providing help that complements or augments what humans are uniquely able to do. The necessary next steps are to engage in further analysis of mobile and intelligent assistance, reflect on the unique roles and qualities of teachers, and collaborate with learners to find optimal ways to assist them and support their learning.

References

Boden, M. A. (2016). *AI: its nature and future*. Oxford University Press.

Dziuban, C., Moskal, P., Johnson, C., & Evans, D. (2017). Adaptive learning: a tale of two contexts. *Current Issues in Emerging eLearning, 4*(1), Article 3. https://scholarworks. umb.edu/ciee/vol4/iss1/3/

Humanium. (2017). *Right to education: situation around the world*. https://www.humanium. org/en/right-to-education/

Kim, H. Y., Kim, B., Jun, S., & Kim, J. (2017, March). An imperfectly perfect robot: discovering interaction design strategy for learning companion. In *Proceedings of 2017 ACM/IEEE International Conference on Human-Robot Interaction* (pp. 165-166). ACM. https://doi.org/10.1145/3029798.3038360

Kukulska-Hulme, A. (2016). Mobile assistance in language learning: a critical appraisal. In A. Palalas & M. Ally (Eds), *The International Handbook of Mobile-Assisted Language Learning* (pp. 138-160). China Central Radio & TV University Press.

Kukulska-Hulme, A., Gaved, M., Paletta, L., Scanlon, E., Jones, A. , & Brasher, A. (2015). Mobile incidental learning to support the inclusion of recent immigrants. *Ubiquitous Learning: an international journal, 7*(2), 9-21.

Li, J., Kizilcec, R., Bailenson, J., & Ju, W. (2016). Social robots and virtual agents as lecturers for video instruction. *Computers in Human Behavior, 55*, 1222-1230. https://doi. org/10.1016/j.chb.2015.04.005

Macedonia, M., Groher, I., & Roithmayr, F. (2014). Intelligent virtual agents as language trainers facilitate multilingualism. *Frontiers in Psychology, 5*. https://doi.org/10.3389/ fpsyg.2014.00295

Philp, J. (2017). *What do successful language learners and their teachers do?* Part of the Cambridge Papers in ELT series. Cambridge University Press. http://cambridge.org/ betterlearning

Scanlon, E., McAndrew, P., & O'Shea, T. (2015). Designing for educational technology to enhance the experience of learners in distance education: how open educational resources, learning design and MOOCs are influencing learning. *Journal of Interactive Media in Education, 1*(6), pp. 1-9. http://dx.doi.org/10.5334/jime.al

UN. (2017). *Sustainable Development goals - ensure inclusive and quality education for all and promote lifelong learning.* United Nations. http://www.un.org/sustainabledevelopment/education/

UNESCO. (2015). *Education for all 2000-2015: achievements and challenges.* EFA Global Monitoring Report. United Nations Educational, Scientific and Cultural Organization. http://unesdoc.unesco.org/images/0023/002322/232205e.pdf

UNESCO. (2017a). *Education and gender equality.* United Nations Educational, Scientific and Cultural Organization. https://en.unesco.org/themes/education-and-gender-equality

UNESCO. (2017b). *Supporting teachers with mobile technology.* United Nations Educational, Scientific and Cultural Organization. http://unesdoc.unesco.org/images/0025/002515/251511e.pdf

UNHCR. (2016). *Missing out: refugee education in crisis.* http://www.unhcr.org/57d9d01d0.pdf

Von Radowitz, J. (2017). *Intelligent machines will replace teachers within 10 years, leading public school headteacher predicts.* Independent newspaper, 11 September 2017. http://www.independent.co.uk/news/education/education-news/intelligent-machines-replace-teachers-classroom-10-years-ai-robots-sir-anthony-sheldon-wellington-a7939931.html

World Bank. (2017). *Girls' education.* http://www.worldbank.org/en/topic/girlseducation

2 MOOCs as a new technology: approaches to normalising the MOOC experience for our learners

Stephen Bax[1]

Abstract

MOOCs (Massive Open Online Courses) are currently in favour as a mechanism for 'delivering education' on a massive scale, including language education. However, when viewed as a new educational 'technology', they have arguably not yet reached the stage of normalisation (Bax, 2003) at which they might be most productive. This paper examines the current landscape with regard to language learning MOOCs, drawing on a number of successful Open University projects in Spanish and Italian. It looks critically at where MOOCs seem to be potentially most valuable, and also at aspects of the experience which seem to have impeded normalisation. The paper will conclude by looking at how language MOOCs might develop in the years ahead.

Keywords: MOOCs, LMOOCs, normalisation, CALL, research, Spanish, language learning.

1. Introduction

I have been discussing normalisation in CALL (Computer Assisted Language Learning) for a number of years (Bax, 2003, Bax, 2011a). Technological innovations do not always become normalised, there are numerous examples

---

1. Paper posthumously transcribed by Marina Orsini-Jones from the plenary given by Stephen Bax at the BMELTT symposium, with the permission of his family.

How to cite this chapter: Bax, S. (2018). MOOCs as a new technology: approaches to normalising the MOOC experience for our learners; paper posthumously transcribed by Marina Orsini-Jones. In M. Orsini-Jones & S. Smith (Eds), *Flipping the blend through MOOCs, MALL and OIL – new directions in CALL* (pp. 9-16). Research-publishing.net. https://doi.org/10.14705/rpnet.2018.23.785

of new technologies that failed and were not adopted widely. I define normalisation as: "the stage when the technology becomes invisible, embedded in everyday practice"; "the stage when a technology is [...] hardly even recognised as a technology, taken for granted in everyday life" (Bax, 2003, p. 23). A recent example of this normalisation is the mobile phone, an older one the humble pen.

In illustrating how normalisation is achieved, I have referred to two factors that can hinder the process through which technologies are adopted: excessive 'awe' (see also Murray & Barnes, 1998 on this point) and excessive 'fear' (see the numerous catastrophic reports on the alleged harmfulness of mobile phones in the press). As mentioned elsewehere,

> "these twin features of excessive 'awe' and exaggerated 'fear' when dealing with new or normalising technologies serve to exemplify the way in which the relationship between technology and society is frequently conceived in popular accounts, namely in absurdly simplistic and polarised terms" (Bax, 2011b, p. 2).

As I have previously argued (Bax, 2011a), when we ask ourselves how a technology can become normalised, it is advisable to seek to answer that question taking into account a number of broader interlocking factors, sociocultural as well as technical. This in turn means that we should set the debate on normalisation within a resolutely social constructivist 'contextualist' framework. For example, chopsticks are normalised technology in China, but not in many other countries. Following Mercer and Fisher's suggestion, I proposed the adoption of a 'Neo-Vygotskian' perspective to the assessment of the normalisation on technology in language education:

> "[t]he essence of this approach is to treat learning and cognitive development as culturally based, not just culturally influenced, and as social rather than individualised processes. It highlights communicative aspects of learning, whereby knowledge is shared and understandings are constructed in culturally formed settings" (Mercer & Fisher, 1997, p. 13, cited in Bax, 2011a, p. 6).

The key points to address in the normalisation process of technology for language education are:

- learning is the priority: the focus must be on fostering language learning, not on technology;

- technology is, in its place, the servant and not the master; and

- beyond 'wow': technology should not be revered, no matter how impressive it appears to be.

Normalisation appears to follow these phases:

- early adopters;

- ignorance/scepticism;

- try once ('no relative advantage' Rogers, 1995);

- try again;

- fear/awe/excessive dependence;

- normalising; and

- normalisation.

It must be pointed out that the above phases do not necessarily follow one from the other and the process of normalisation is not automatic. It does not happen with all technologies – sometimes they are not normalised and are not used. With virtually every new technology there is a fear about the dangers. With reference to MOOCs, I would argue that we are at Stage 5, still quite a way from normalisation. I have encountered both awe and fear when discussing MOOCs with language educators. MOOCs are seen by some as the revolution to learning and development. Some progress in researching the affordances and applications of MOOCs has been made and there are new publications that help with framing how MOOCs can be utilised in language education (e.g. Kan & Bax, 2017), but there are some fundamental questions that we need to ask on the way to normalisation;

- Are MOOCs normalised?
    - For learners?
    - For teachers?
    - For administrators?
    - For all the stakeholders or just some of them?

- Is normalisation for MOOCs desirable? (As we are in the "awe" stage, of course we think it is desirable – but is this a true reflection?).

- How can we achieve it?

- What obstacles lie in the way?

A critical appraisal of MOOCs for language education is needed, that goes beyond the 'wow' factor (Bax, 2011b; Murray & Barnes, 1998) to ascertain if it is desirable that MOOCs become normalised and, if it is, what shape and form should a good MOOC for language education have.

2.   Key features of MOOCs

MOOCs are, as their acronym states, massive, open, and online. Quite often there is low tutor/student interaction, for obvious reasons: there might be 50,000 students and 20 tutors (see Figure 1: Participants' numbers of the Spanish MOOC by The Open University). So there normally are less opportunities for interaction than in a language classroom or even in a well-attended lecture. For similar reasons, the mode of learning is transmission of knowledge on a MOOC, as it is easier to put information on a MOOC that is accessed by participants rather than engage in interaction with 50,000 participants, ask them questions, and obtain feedback from them. Although there is some social dimension to a MOOC, as there are forums for example, the opportunity for interaction is reduced in comparison with a face-to-face classroom setting.

Figure 1.   Participants' numbers of the Spanish MOOC by The Open University on FutureLearn[2]

Spanish for Beginners 1: Meeting and Greeting

Datasets	Overview	Totals	Weekly

Filter stats up to a date:

23 Oct 2016   16 Oct 2016   9 Oct 2016   2 Oct 2016   25 Sep 2016   18 Sep 2016

Course Run Measures

Accurate up to midnight on 24 October 2016

Joiners	49,120	
Leavers	2,825	5.8%
Learners	31,918	65.0%
Active Learners	28,315	88.7%
Returning Learners	11,049	34.6%
Social Learners	9,786	30.7%
Fully Participating Learners	4,903	15.4%

I propose to evaluate where we are with MOOCs and where we should be from a theoretical perspective. In this context, it is useful to refer back to an old, but still valid, framework by Jane Willis (1996), who classifies the key areas of language learning in four points, or conditions. Willis (1996) states that three are essential:

- **exposure** (which I would call **input**) to a rich but comprehensible input of real spoken and written language in use;

---

2. Reproduced with kind permissions from the copyright holder.

- **use** of the language to do things (i.e. exchange meanings, which I would call **output**);

- **motivation** to listen to, read, speak, and write the language (i.e. to process and use the exposure).

Willis (1996) also adds a fourth, which she calls desirable: **instruction in the language** (i.e. chances to **focus on form**).

I agree with Willis (1996) that these four areas are fundamental to language learning, but would propose to move them around. Motivation comes first for me, how the learner feels about the learning that is taking place, the 'affect' – the will that you have towards the subject you are studying. A language learner is unlikely to learn a language if they hate their teacher and/or the language they are learning. Secondly comes input: the quantity and quality of it. Quality includes the range of language input, so a student who is focusing on conversational Italian will not be able to read Dante, unless they are exposed to a wide range of language. Likewise, output needs to consist of good opportunities for speaking and writing, the third aspect. Fourthly, focus on form should relate to feedback – the importance of focusing on where you went wrong. I do not see this aspect of language learning as optional, like Willis does, but rather that it forms an integral part of the language learning process.

If we look for these four factors in Language MOOCs (LMOOCs), we can see that LMOOCs score quite high on motivations, they can be fun, but sometimes the experience can be a bit isolated and the student will need support. The evaluation of the Open University's LMOOCs delivered on the FutureLearn platform illustrates that the affective point is well addressed by MOOCs, possibly also because they are still relatively new ('wow' factor). Input is also good on LMOOCs, even considering their interactional limitations and the lack of exposure to genre variety in them. There are, however, problems with output and feedback. It is difficult to practise output (speaking and writing) on a MOOC and obtain feedback on one's production. These are essential factors in language learning and LMOOCs have serious shortcomings in these two areas.

3.   Conclusions and recommendations

The limitations of the LMOOCs identified above can hinder their normalisation. If students think they can learn a whole language from a MOOC students will become dissatisfied, attendance on LMOOCs might decline and 'massive' might become 'miniscule' as a consequence of this. If the expectation is too high to start with there is a serious danger of it failing.

So what can we do? Firstly it is necessary to cast a critical eye on LMOOCs, paying attention to their shortcomings to see how they can be resolved or circumvented through research, design, and operation. It is recommended to go beyond the 'wow' factor and manage the expectations of students. LMOOCs are not a panacea for language learning, not the whole solution, only a part of it. That is the usual problem with new technologies, that some people start to think that new technologies can solve all their problems. This is the lesson learnt from research into normalisation. Students must be supported in accessing additional listening and speaking elements, for example, and/or be provided them as extras outside the LMOOCs. If this is not done, LMOOCs might die the same death that some other rather unusual technologies died, before becoming normalised.

It is also important to carry out more research on MOOCs and examples of this are provided in Kan and Bax (2017). We must also think about the design and operation of MOOCs to take account of gaps and shortcomings we might identify. Some of this LMOOC research has for example informed the design of the FutureLearn Spanish for Beginners LMOOC. Learners' perceptions of LMOOCs must be studied and must inform their design.

In summary:

- MOOCs are not yet normalised;

- normalisation requires more research, leading to planning, then more research;

- research: focus on obstacles to normalisation;

- research: based on language learning theory/research base;

- identify gaps;

- then plan for the gaps, and alternatives; and

- raise awareness of learners and teachers of the limitations of the MOOCs and encourage them to take action to resolve the issues/lacks and wants.

References

Bax, S. (2003). CALL—past, present and future. *System, 31*(1), 13-28. https://doi.org/10.1016/S0346-251X(02)00071-4

Bax, S. (2011a). Normalisation revisited: the effective use of technology in language education. *IJCALLT, 1*(2), 1-15. https://doi.org/10.4018/ijcallt.2011040101

Bax, S. (2011b). Digital education: beyond the "wow" factor. In M. Thomas (Ed.), *Digital education.* Palgrave Macmillan's Digital Education and Learning. https://doi.org/10.1057/9780230118003_12

Bax, S. (2017). *MOOCs as a new technology: approaches to normalising the MOOCs experience for our learners.* Paper presented at the B-MELTT: Flipping the Blend through MALL, MOOCs and BOIL – New Directions in CALL Symposium, Coventry, UK: Coventry University. https://youtu.be/S1ZJf74HxnA

Kan, Q., & Bax, S. (Eds). (2017). *Beyond the language classroom: researching MOOCs and other innovations.* Research-publishing.net. https://doi.org/10.14705/rpnet.2017.mooc2016.9781908416537

Mercer, N., & Fisher, E. (1997). The importance of talk. In R. Wegerif & P. Scrimshaw (Eds), *Computers and talk in the primary classroom* (pp. 13-21). Multilingual Matters.

Murray, L., & Barnes, A. (1998). Beyond the "wow" factor—evaluating multimedia language learning software from a pedagogical viewpoint. *System, 26*, 249-259.

Rogers, E. (1995). *Diffusion of innovations.* Free Press.

Willis, J. (1996). *A framework for task-based learning.* Longman.

3 What our MOOC did next: embedding, exploiting, and extending an existing MOOC to fit strategic purposes and priorities

Kate Borthwick[1]

Abstract

This chapter describes how one particular Massive Open Online Course (MOOC), created at the University of Southampton, has evolved beyond its core purpose as a promotional tool, to complement and serve purposes and priorities of relevance and importance to wider university strategic aims. It briefly outlines elements of the course design and content, and the impact of the course over its six runs to date. It describes the steps taken to shape the evolution of the course including review, re-use of assets, use of the course in research, and its role as inspiration for a 'spin-off' course. It concludes by noting that one MOOC can provide rich and varied opportunities to enhance and support areas which are key priorities in UK higher education institutions.

Keywords: MOOC, language learning, online education, blended learning.

1. Introduction and background

Research into the development of MOOCs from essentially standalone educational experiences toward utilisation more widely as part of a broader

1. University of Southampton, Southampton, United Kingdom; k.borthwick@soton.ac.uk

How to cite this chapter: Borthwick, K. (2018). What our MOOC did next: embedding, exploiting, and extending an existing MOOC to fit strategic purposes and priorities. In M. Orsini-Jones & S. Smith (Eds), *Flipping the blend through MOOCs, MALL and OIL – new directions in CALL* (pp. 17-23). Research-publishing.net. https://doi.org/10.14705/rpnet.2018.23.786

approach to education has been underway for some years. In 2014, a CETIS[2] white paper identified MOOCs as an opportunity for institutions to think more strategically about online education given their potential for "enhancing existing classroom teaching practices, promoting institutional reputation, and developing new revenue models" (Yuan, Powell, & Olivier, 2014, p. 3). Since that time, MOOCs have been incorporated into the digital strategies of many universities in the UK, for example, the University of Edinburgh describes MOOCs as part of its "commitment to knowledge exchange and outreach"[3], and University College London makes use of them as short, professional development courses within a community of learners and researchers[4]. There is also a growing body of work being developed on how MOOCs might contribute to campus-based teaching through blended learning scenarios (e.g. Israel, 2015; Orsini-Jones, 2015).

The University of Southampton's major involvement with MOOCs began in 2013, when it became one of FutureLearn's[5] first partners. FutureLearn Ltd was created with the intention of becoming the UK's primary MOOC-platform provider and it has been highly successful in doing this, and in encouraging the development of high-quality, appealing online courses. It currently boasts over seven million learners and continues to grow. Since 2013, the University of Southampton has created 18 different courses via FutureLearn which have had circa 80 runs (at time of writing). These courses have reached over 630,000 learners[6]. Although most Southampton MOOCs were originally developed as standalone online courses, our MOOC teams across the university have sought to explore how such courses can support campus-based activities in diverse ways, from outreach and recruitment activities to blending MOOCs with campus-based education.

---

2. Centre for Educational Technology, Interoperability and Standards, United Kingdom; http://www.cetis.org.uk/

3. https://www.ed.ac.uk/studying/moocs/about

4. http://www.ucl.ac.uk/ioe/courses/short-courses-cpd/moocs

5. www.futurelearn.com; https://www.futurelearn.com/courses/understanding-language

6. Number of learners signed up to UoS/FL courses, as of December 2017.

Considerations around the evolution of Southampton MOOCs has taken place against the backdrop of the implementation of a revised institutional strategy entitled 'Simply Better'[7], which emphasises (amongst other aspects) the consolidation, extension, and promotion of excellence in research, teaching, and enterprise.

2. Method

The focus of this chapter is a MOOC that was initially developed in 2014, called 'Understanding Language: learning and teaching'[8]. This course was created as a collaboration between Modern Languages and Linguistics at Southampton and the British Council[9] and it was intended to act primarily as a marketing tool to increase student recruitment to a jointly run online Masters (MA) in English Language Teaching (ELT)[10]. It offers a 'taste' of key concepts in the study of applied linguistics and runs over four weeks, featuring a different topic each week: language learning, language teaching, technology in teaching, and Global English. Course content reflects some activities and topics covered in the Masters in ELT. The course has attracted over 100,000 learners over 6 runs[11].

Course content is delivered by a range of staff within applied linguistics at Southampton and at the British Council via short videos and linked discussion questions. It aims to be academic but approachable in tone. There are also texts to read, tasks to engage in, and interactive elements such as polls. Learners discuss and respond to questions or tasks in comment areas attached to each activity and the notion of 'learning as a conversation' is at the core of the learning design[12].

---

7. https://www.southampton.ac.uk/about/strategy.page

8. www.futurelearn.com/courses/understanding-language

9. www.britishcouncil.org

10. https://www.southampton.ac.uk/humanities/postgraduate/taught_courses/taught_courses/modern_languages/r900_ma_english_language_teaching_online.page

11. Learners are defined by FutureLearn as people who have signed up and viewed at least one step.

12. https://www.futurelearn.com/using-futurelearn/why-it-works

Peer learning through social activity is a key part of the course's design and activities frequently require learners to share their own content, e.g. photographs of their own classrooms or plotting their global location on an interactive map. The course is greatly enriched by the shared experiences and knowledge contributed by learners.

Tutoring on the course is offered by a mix of university and British Council staff, who monitor comments and respond with questions, comments, and further information. One of the key roles of a tutor is to foster the development of conversations around course concepts and topics. Such ongoing activity is complemented by more high profile tutor input in the form of end-of-week video reviews, which summarise key discussions and respond to learner questions raised during the week.

3.   Results and impact

3.1.   Number of learners

The course has generated a great deal of interest globally with consistently high numbers of learners signing up to take it at each run. Naturally, numbers have dropped over time but are still healthy: 58,000+ for the first run compared to 10,000+ for the sixth run. Of those that sign up to take the course, on average 50% actually click through to start the course. The vast majority of learners on the course are from outside the UK. A related Youtube channel which hosts tutor reviews and recordings of live content has had over 79,000 views.

3.2.   Recruitment to online MA in ELT

There has been an increase in numbers applying for the online MA in ELT and the cohort has increased in size over several recruitment cycles and become more geographically spread across the globe. During the first run of the MOOC, a scholarship scheme was piloted which offered the opportunity to apply for a discount on fees for the MA to learners who completed the MOOC. This generated a large amount of interest (circa 8000 expressions of interest) and so the scheme has been maintained throughout all of the course runs, resulting in a number of scholarship students within the MA cohort.

3.3. Impact on local staff

There has also been a positive impact on academic staff who have contributed content to the MOOC. Engagement with creating the MOOC has led them to consider how aspects of MOOC/FutureLearn pedagogy might feed back into classroom-based teaching (e.g. focused, bite-size input leading to a conversational approach); how the communication of complex ideas could be presented in clear and accessible ways without losing academic rigour; and how accessing new audiences beyond the classroom walls could be a highly rewarding experience.

4. Evolution over time

4.1. Re-use of MOOC digital assets

The course was edited ahead of each new run in line with user and tutor feedback and experienced a major review ahead of its fifth run. This review saw content edited and updated, links added, some structural changes (the rationalisation of some activity steps) and the addition of an extra week (see below). Staff within applied linguistics were encouraged to use disaggregated MOOC content to support campus-based classes by adding materials to the University's virtual learning environment.

4.2. MOOC as research instrument

For the fifth run of the course, an extra week was added. The purpose of this was to provide updates to the fast-moving field of Global English and to experiment with using the course to crowd-source research data about language policies and practices around the world. The research data would feed into an existing international research project led by Professor Jennifer Jenkins, the Director of the Centre for Global Englishes at Southampton. The course offered an excellent opportunity to capture a diversity of perspectives on the global use of English, due to the high number of globally-located course participants using English as a second language.

The new week invited learners to take part in a survey about language policies in their local context and thus to become part of an extended research and education community by contributing to ongoing research. The response has been excellent and the survey was closed after more than 1000 responses. Data is still being analysed and will form a key part of the research team's work going forward.

4.3. Next generation MOOC

The team's experience in creating and delivering the MOOC has inspired the creation of another FutureLearn course: English as a Medium of Instruction for Academics[13]. The course builds on ideas touched upon in week 4 of 'Understanding Language' and is oriented toward the continuing professional development of teachers in higher education. The focus of the course is around working effectively in international classrooms, discussing linguistic and cultural issues, and complementing the ideas covered by the earlier MOOC. 'EMI for Academics' was created as a MOOC, but will be repurposed and run internally for our own staff alongside classroom-based workshops.

5. Conclusions

The MOOC 'Understanding Language: learning and teaching' was created with an explicit marketing or enterprise-related purpose and it has been successful in this core purpose. It has also proved to be a rich educational experience for thousands for learners and inspiring for the staff involved in its creation. It has

---

13. https://www.futurelearn.com/courses/emi-academics

piloted and supported an innovative way to collect research data and the re-use of its high quality digital materials have led to improved support for campus-based students. It has taken excellence in research and teaching to a global audience. In these respects, it demonstrates the rich potential that just one open online course can offer to enhance and support areas important to higher education: research, education, enterprise, outreach, and student engagement. As the course continues to run, we will continue to seek opportunities to align it further with university priorities and this will include reviewing its effectiveness and development as a promotional tool to attract new students. These activities will take place as part of a vision of online education which is very appealing: not a distinct and separate activity but integrated into the fabric of university business and life.

Acknowledgements

The MOOC described here – and its ongoing delivery and development – is the work of a large number of people working at the University of Southampton and the British Council: my thanks go to all of them for their continued dedication and hard work to its success. No less important are the learners on the course, who make 'Understanding Language' a wonderfully enjoyable and rewarding experience, and who never fail to inspire us every time the course runs.

References

Israel, M. J. (2015). Effectiveness of integrating MOOCs in traditional classrooms for undergraduate students. *International Review of Research in Open and Distributed Learning, 16*(5). https://doi.org/10.19173/irrodl.v16i5.2222

Orsini-Jones, M. (2015). *Integrating a MOOC into the MA in english language teaching at Coventry University: innovation in blended learning practice.* Higher Education Academy. https://www.heacademy.ac.uk/system/files/marina_orsini_jones_final_1.pdf

Yuan, L., Powell, S., & Olivier, B. (2014). *Beyond MOOCs: sustainable online learning in institutions.* A white paper for the Centre for Educational Technology, Interoperability and Standards. http://publications.cetis.ac.uk/2014/898

4 Integrating a MOOC into the MA curriculum: an 'expert' student's reflections on blended learning

Minh Tuan Phi[1]

Abstract

Autonomy is a highly debated concept in the field of language learning and teaching. It is argued here that the integration of Massive Open Online Courses (MOOCs) in tertiary education can help language teachers and learners to address this troublesome concept. This paper reports on the learning journey of a Master of Arts (MA) in English Language Teaching and Applied Linguistics (MAELTAL) student at Coventry University (CU). It discusses autonomy and blended learning in language learning and teaching in the context of engaging with the FutureLearn MOOC *Understanding Language: Learning and Teaching* integrated into the MAELTAL curriculum. This report explores how a blended MOOC approach impacted on the MAELTAL student's beliefs and his identity as an autonomous teacher of English.

Keywords: reflection, learner autonomy, teacher autonomy, blended learning, MOOC.

---

1. Introduction

I am an English language teacher from Hanoi, Vietnam. I obtained my Bachelor Degree in International Economics at the Diplomatic Academy of Vietnam.

---

1. University of Coventry, Coventry, United Kingdom; minhtuanphi@hotmail.com

How to cite this chapter: Phi, M. T. (2018). Integrating a MOOC into the MA curriculum: an 'expert' student's reflections on blended learning . In M. Orsini-Jones & S. Smith (Eds), *Flipping the blend through MOOCs, MALL and OIL – new directions in CALL* (pp. 25-31). Research-publishing.net. https://doi.org/10.14705/rpnet.2018.23.787

During my undergraduate study, I worked as an English private tutor for IELTS candidates. That part-time job fuelled my desire to become an English teacher. In 2013, I became an English assistant lecturer in Hanoi Open University, where I worked under a module leader's supervision to give lectures on General English and Academic English. This job provided me motivation to further my study at CU, where I completed my MA in English Language Teaching and Applied Linguistics in 2017. I had never engaged with a MOOC before the MA study, and the concept of autonomy in language learning and teaching was completely alien to me. However, engaging with a FutureLearn MOOC complimented my study on the MA course in that my learning was consolidated through the learning material which was presented in various ways and from a variety of different perspectives at no extra cost.

The FutureLearn MOOC *Understanding Language: Learning and Teaching* was embedded as an open educational "extra line of support" into the compulsory module named *Theories and Methods of Language Learning and Teaching* at CU (Orsini-Jones et al., 2015). According to Orsini-Jones (2015), it provided the opportunity for MAELTAL students to explore how Learner Autonomy (LA) could be developed through the engagement with a face-to-face module blended with an online course.

Students were required to record their reflections during each week throughout the five-week duration of the FutureLearn MOOC, and then shared their meta-reflections on a weekly basis on the CU Open Moodle platform. At the end of the module, students were assessed through an optional question on their experience of involvement with the FutureLearn MOOC in relation to LA in English language learning and teaching. This question was incorporated into the summative assessment via the in-class test (see Orsini-Jones, 2015, for further information on how the FutureLearn MOOC was blended into the MA programme).

This auto-ethnographic report focuses, therefore, on the reflections concerning my own experience of engaging with the FutureLearn MOOC throughout my MA study at CU.

2.   The FutureLearn MOOC blend
at Coventry University

Various studies (Orsini-Jones, 2015; Reinders & White, 2016) have emphasised
the integral role of technology-based instruction in promoting autonomy.
According to Kleiman, Wolf, and Frye (2015, p. 117), MOOCs have paved the
way for improvements in language teachers' education, focusing on enhancing
their expertise and advancing their professional teaching practices. MOOCs are
supported by Siemens' (2005) idea of connectivism for the digital age. In another
study, Siemens (2012) characterises the distinct feature in designing MOOCs as
knowledge that can be co-constructed. The language learners are engaged in a
"technological-supported environment that supports meaningful dialogue and
collaboration" (Kizito, 2016) to "connect and form information and knowledge
sources" (Bartolome & Steffens, 2015, p. 96).

Ragan (2007) defines the concept of blended learning as "the planned integration
of online and face-to-face instructional approaches in a way that maximises the
positive features of each respective delivery mode". This form of MOOC blend,
in which the content plays an integral part in an existing curriculum, is relatively
new in tertiary education in the UK (Orsini-Jones, Gafaro, & Altamimi, 2017).
Such courses, Picciano, Dziuban, and Graham (2014, p. 3) propose, are also
known as 'mixed-mode learning', or 'hybrid learning'. Within this teaching
approach, not only do language teachers employ technology-enabled teaching
materials on the internet to improve their teaching efficiency and effectiveness,
but they also prepare their students ahead of time for the traditional teaching
methods (Larson & Murray, 2008). According to Sandeen (2013), blending a
MOOC into a part of the higher education programmes can "enable campus
faculty to retain a high degree of control over course content and the granting of
credit recognition" (p. 36). Bonk and Khoo (2014) believe the engagement with
MOOCs as parts of the traditional curricula may foster an autonomous approach
to language learning (pp. 156-158).

The FutureLearn MOOC blend I experienced at CU was accompanied by
classroom teaching lessons. MAELTAL students could find similar topics which

were equivalent to the face-to-face lessons in class - such as task-based language learning and teaching and Content and Language Integrated Learning (CLIL). This gave students more assistance in understanding the pedagogical themes they learned on the MA module. For instance, I was not fully aware of what CLIL was until I watched the relevant videos on week 2 of the FutureLearn MOOC. The videos and the tasks on the FutureLearn MOOC could be considered as a good preparation that helped me comprehend the lesson in class. In addition, The FutureLearn MOOC shares the principle of mobile learning – studying "anytime", "anywhere", suggested by Kukulska-Hulme and Shield (2008, p. 281). According to Hood, Littlejohn, and Milligan (2015), the MOOC blend allows participants to self-regulate their own learning journey. Therefore, MAELTAL students could complete their studies at their own pace, which represents an individualised approach to adaptive learning.

Not only did the MOOC blend I took part in at CU provide MAELTAL students an opportunity to engage with the global community of practice on the MOOC, it was also amplified by the face-to-face seminars and the online knowledge-sharing exchange on the CU Open Moodle platform with CU partners in China and the Netherlands, as part of an added Online International Learning (OIL) project funded by the British Council (English language teaching research funding). The exploratory study carried out by Orsini-Jones et al. (2015), which discussed the experience of engaging with the MOOC, emphasised that the communication on the FutureLearn MOOC forums was difficult to follow since there were too many comments. The question of how best to structure the MOOC blend's online discussions to maximise social co-construction of knowledge was then answered by designing a dedicated CU Moodle platform. This is in line with what is suggested by Coetzee et al. (2015) who emphasise the use of small peer groups to support MOOC participants in their learning of content and reflection on their progress. Furthermore, the online international exchange was then followed and reinforced by a joint staff/student conference on the FutureLearn MOOC organised during a study visit to the Netherlands in April 2017 to meet the OIL partners. The MAELTAL students at CU had the opportunity to discuss their learning journey on the FutureLearn MOOC in a "meta-blended approach" proposed by Orsini-Jones (2015), including: (1)

within the blended learning setting at CU; (2) online with a globally connected discussion forum on teaching and learning via the FutureLearn MOOC website; (3) online with their peers on the CU Open Moodle platform; and (4) face-to-face with their peers in the Netherlands.

However, the FutureLearn MOOC also had some negative aspects. Orsini-Jones et al. (2015, p. 455) note that MOOCs lack the presence of teachers "supporting the learners at each step they take". MAELTAL students might find it easier to interact face-to-face rather than on MOOCs' online discussion. Israel (2015, p. 112) emphasises the fact that the level of participation on MOOCs can decline due to the feeling of isolation produced by the absence of tutors.

3.   Conclusions

The blending of advanced technology in English language learning and teaching is opening new horizons for LA and Teacher Autonomy (TA) (Cappellini, Lewis, & Rivens Mompean, 2017). Autonomous pedagogical teaching approaches can be promoted through an integration of conventional/formal/face-to-face and informal/distance learning settings, for instance by blending MOOCs into existing curricula (Orsini-Jones, Zou, Borthwick, & Garafo, 2017). On a personal level, the MOOC blend that I experienced during my MA studies has certainly transformed my perception of online and blended learning. I have moved from scepticism to conversion and I now believe that a MOOC blend can promote autonomy. I believe that the experience of reflecting on how to teach English with the support of a MOOC blend has also helped me to understand Kumaravadivelu's (2001) post-method philosophy , which encourages "teachers to theorise from their practice and to practice what they theorise".

References

Bartolome, A., & Steffens, K. (2015). Are MOOCs promising learning environments?/¿ Son los MOOC una alternativa de aprendizaje? *Comunicar, 22*(44), 91-99.

Bonk, C. J., & Khoo, E. G. (2014). *Adding some TEC-VARIETY: 100+ activities for motivating and retaining learners online.* Open World Books.

Cappellini, M., Lewis, T., & Rivens Mompean, A. (2017). *Learner autonomy and web 2.0.* Equinox.

Coetzee, D., Lim, S., Fox, A., Hartmann, B., & Hearst, M. A. (2015). Structuring interactions for large-scale synchronous peer learning. *Proceedings of the collaboration in the open classroom conference, 14-18 March 2015, CSCW* (pp. 1139-1152). https://doi. org/10.1145/2675133.2675251

Hood, N., Littlejohn, A., & Milligan, C. (2015). Context counts: how learners' contexts influence learning in a MOOC. *Computers & Education, 91,* 83-91. https://doi. org/10.1016/j.compedu.2015.10.019

Israel, M. J. (2015). Effectiveness of integrating MOOCs in traditional classrooms for undergraduate students. *The International Review of Research in Open and Distributed Learning, 16*(5), 102-118. https://doi.org/10.19173/irrodl.v16i5.2222

Kizito, R. N. (2016). Connectivism in learning activity design: implications for pedagogically-based technology adoption in African higher education contexts. *The International Review of Research in Open and Distributed Learning, 17*(2). https://doi.org/10.19173/irrodl.v17i2.2217

Kleiman, G., Wolf, M., & Frye, D. (2015). Educating educators: designing MOOCs for professional learning. In P. Kim (Ed.), *The MOOC revolution: massive open online courses and the future of education* (pp. 117-146). Routledge.

Kukulska-Hulme, A., & Shield, L. (2008). An overview of mobile assisted language learning: from content delivery to supported collaboration and interaction. *ReCALL, 20,* 271-289. https://doi.org/10.1017/S0958344008000335

Kumaravadivelu, B. (2001). Toward a postmethod pedagogy. *TESOL quarterly, 35,* 537-560. https://doi.org/10.2307/3588427

Larson, R. C., & Murray, M. E. (2008). Open educational resources for blended learning in high schools: overcoming impediments in developing countries. *Journal of Asynchronous Learning Networks, 12,* 85-103. https://doi.org/10.24059/olj.v12i1.52

Orsini-Jones, M. (2015). *Integrating a MOOC into the MA in English language teaching at Coventry University: innovation in blended learning practice.* https://curve.coventry. ac.uk/open/items/f4b0f2b3-147f-4f27-a4d4-67d542083029/1/

Orsini-Jones, M., Gafaro, B. C., & Altamimi, S. (2017). Integrating a MOOC into the postgraduate ELT curriculum: reflecting on students' beliefs with a MOOC blend. In Q. Kan & S. Bax (Eds), *Beyond the language classroom: researching MOOCs and other innovations* (pp. 71-83). Research-publishing.net. https://doi.org/10.14705/rpnet.2017.mooc2016.672

Orsini-Jones, M., Pibworth L., Cribb, M., Brick, B., Gazeley-eke, Z., Leinster, H., & Lloyd, E. (2015). Learning about language learning on a MOOC: how massive, open, online and "course"? In F. Helm, L. Bradley, M. Guarda & S. Thouesny (Eds), *Critical CALL – Proceedings of the 2015 EUROCALL Conference, Padova, Italy, 2015* (pp. 450-457). Research-publishing.net. https://doi.org/10.14705/rpnet.2015.000374

Orsini-Jones, M., Zou, B., Borthwick, K., & Garafo, B. C. (2017). B-MELTT (Blending MOOCs for English Language Teaching Training): a 'Distributed MOOC Flip' to explore local and global ELT contexts and beliefs. In J. Colpaert, A. Aerts, R. Kern & M. Kaiser (Eds), *CALL in context, 2017*. University of California.

Picciano, A. G., Dziuban, C. D., & Graham, C. R. (2014). *Blended learning: research perspectives - Volume 2*. Routledge.

Ragan, L. C. (2007). *Ten principles of effective online teaching: best practices in distance education*. Magna Publications. http://www.facultyfocus.com/free-reports/principles-of-effective-online-teaching-best-practices-in-distance-education/

Reinders, H., & White, C. (2016). 20 years of autonomy and technology: how far have we come and where to next? *Language Learning & Technology, 20*(2), 143-154.

Sandeen, C. (2013). Integrating MOOCs into traditional higher education: the emerging "MOOC 3.0" era. *Change: The magazine of higher learning, 45*, 34-39. https://doi.org/1 0.1080/00091383.2013.842103

Siemens, G. (2005). Connectivism: a learning theory for the digital age. *ElearnSpace, everything elearning*. http://www.elearnspace.org/Articles/connectivism.htm

Siemens, G. (2012). What is the theory that underpins our MOOCs? *ElearnSpace, everything elearning*. http://www.elearnspace.org/blog/2012/06/03/what-is-the-theory-that-underpins-our-moocs/

5 Understanding learner autonomy through MOOC-supported blended learning environments: an investigation into Chinese MA ELT students' beliefs

Yan Jiao[1]

Abstract

This short paper attempts to investigate how the FutureLearn[2] Massive Open Online Course (MOOC) blend, integrated into the module Theories, Methods, and Approaches of Language Learning and Teaching on the Master of Arts (MA) in English Language Teaching and Applied Linguistics at Coventry University, affected Chinese MA students' perceptions of learner autonomy and their teaching practice. The findings are supported by the data collected from an online survey, individual semi-structured interviews, and Video Stimulated Recall (VSR) interviews based on microteaching practices carried out by participants for the module Teaching English in Higher Education. The study identified a gap between experienced teachers' theoretical beliefs on learner autonomy and their microteaching practice, which could be influenced by their prior teaching experience in the traditional teacher-centred Chinese educational context.

Keywords: learner autonomy, beliefs, practice, MOOC-supported blended learning environment, chinese ELT students.

1. Coventry University, Coventry, United Kingdom; jiaoy6@uni.coventry.ac.uk

2. www.futurelearn.com

How to cite this chapter: Jiao, Y. (2018). Understanding learner autonomy through MOOC-supported blended learning environments: an investigation into Chinese MA ELT students' beliefs. In M. Orsini-Jones & S. Smith (Eds), *Flipping the blend through MOOCs, MALL and OIL – new directions in CALL* (pp. 33-40). Research-publishing.net. https://doi.org/10.14705/rpnet.2018.23.788

1.   Introduction

The shift from teacher-centred to student-centred teaching could motivate learners to take more responsibility for their learning process and embrace their new identity as autonomous learners. Benson (2006) reports on various studies illustrating that learner autonomy has a significant role to play in successful foreign language learning. However, in some traditional teacher-centred learning cultures, the learner responsibility has been suppressed or ignored (Armstrong, 2012, p. 2426). Littlewood (1999) argues that there are different degrees of autonomy, such as a higher level of autonomy (i.e. proactive autonomy) and a lower level of autonomy (i.e. reactive autonomy).

Proactive autonomy refers to the kind of autonomy which is generally mentioned in Western learning cultures, where learners are often encouraged to take control of their own learning process (Littlewood, 1999, p. 75). On the other hand, reactive autonomy "does not create its own directions but, once a direction has been initiated, it enables learners to organise their resources autonomously in order to reach their goal" (Littlewood 1999, p. 75), which is discussed in East Asian learning cultures.

Furthermore, Littlewood (1999, cited in Gieve & Clark, 2005, p. 262) points out that traditional "Confucian attitudes to learning and teaching" have resulted in the teacher-centred class in China where teachers are generally the primary source of knowledge. Therefore, there could be a mismatch between Chinese English Language Teaching (ELT) students' perceptions of learner autonomy (i.e. reactive autonomy) and the generally recognised notion of learner autonomy (i.e. proactive autonomy) in Western educational cultures.

These reflections have emerged from the "apparent differences between British and Chinese cultures of learning" (Jin & Cortazzi, 1993, 1996, cited in Gieve & Clark, 2005, p. 2). It is argued here that the mismatch in the understanding of the concept of learner autonomy between Western and Eastern learning cultures means that Chinese students studying this concept in the UK while engaging in teacher education find it 'troublesome' (Meyer & Land, 2003). Orsini-Jones

(2015) discusses the complexities of the concept of learner autonomy for students engaging in teacher education and suggests that it could be a "threshold concept". Threshold Concepts (TCs) (Meyer & Land, 2003) challenge the belief system of learners. They are concepts of fundamental importance in a subject which, if understood, can open new learning horizons and help to grasp other related troublesome knowledge. The encounter with a TC can lead to a state of "liminality", i.e. the oscillation between grasping the concept and the feeling that it is out of reach (Meyer & Land, 2006, p. 22). Crossing the TC allows learners to access "a new and previously inaccessible way of thinking about something" (Meyer & Land, 2006, p. 3), which results in an ontological (transformation affecting the "being") and epistemological (transformation at the level of knowledge and language) shift.

Gieve and Clark (2005) argue that it is possible for students from traditional learning cultures to become autonomous learners, as long as they are exposed to autonomy-supportive environments. The adoption of blended learning could be an effective approach to providing Chinese ELT learners with autonomy-supportive environments. According to Orsini-Jones (2015), blending a FutureLearn MOOC into the formal curriculum could assist international students to manage the above-mentioned troublesome knowledge and develop their autonomy. In the study reported here, the FutureLearn MOOC *Exploring the World of English Language Teaching* was blended into the formal curriculum of the MA in English Language Teaching and Applied Linguistic (ELTAL) at Coventry University. Students were invited to engage in reflective practice on their beliefs as teachers while doing the MOOC. They engaged in weekly reflections on how engaging with ELT topics online was affecting their understanding of both learner and teacher autonomy and of how new technologies could be integrated into the ELT learning process.

This study aims to investigate how the MOOC blend implemented on the MA in ELT and Applied Linguistics at Coventry University influences Chinese ELT students' beliefs on learner autonomy and whether or not such theoretical beliefs are applied in practice when delivering the assessed micro-teaching task for the MA.

2.   Methodology

This study was carried out according to the ethics procedures at Coventry University, which are Data Protection Act compliant. Informed consent was sought from all self-selected participants. A qualitative approach was adopted that included the administration of a Bristol Online Survey[3], semi-structured individual interviews, and VSR interviews. The following research questions were addressed:

- How do Chinese ELT students perceive themselves as autonomous learners before and after taking part in the FutureLearn MOOC blended learning project?

- What aspects of the FutureLearn MOOC blended learning project have influenced the Chinese ELT students' perceptions on learner autonomy?

- To what extent do Chinese ELT students' perceptions of learner autonomy align with their actual practices to promote learner autonomy?

3.   Results and Discussion

3.1.   Research question 1

The findings from surveys and semi-structured interviews revealed that all of the four participants were not given opportunities to practise their learner autonomy (i.e. proactive autonomy) when they were studying or teaching in China, instead they practised and fostered reactive autonomy (i.e. a lower level of autonomy), which could be a result of the Asian educational culture they have experienced (Littlewood, 1999). After engaging with the MOOC blended learning project, a sociocultural dimension (Little, 1995) of learner autonomy was mentioned by

---

3. https://www.onlinesurveys.ac.uk

all of the participants[4], which is also a characteristic of Eastern learning cultures regarding collectivism (Littlewood, 1999). Furthermore, an independent dimension of learner autonomy (Littlewood, 1999) was highlighted by two of the participants with little teaching experience. However, the data collected from the surveys illustrated that the four participants still had a tendency to believe that teachers are responsible for the learning process[5]. This possibly derives from their traditional teacher-centred educational culture (Chang & Holt, 1994; Wang, 2008). Thus, the findings indicate that these Chinese ELT students experienced "a state of 'liminality' within the threshold" (Land, Cousin, Meyer, & Davies, 2005, p. 55). In other words, they were reluctant to relinquish their previous "comfortable positions" (Land et al., 2005, p. 54) and accept the shift in their identity (Orsini-Jones, Conde Gafaro, & Altamimi, 2017, p. 8).

3.2. Research question 2

The participants were asked to reflect on and compare their learning experience on the FutureLearn MOOC and face-to-face lecturers in order to identify the aspects which influenced their beliefs on learner autonomy. Most of the participants stated that the FutureLearn MOOC was beneficial to them[6]. Furthermore, the data collected from individual interviews revealed that activities (e.g. group discussions, meta-reflective practices) carried out in the face-to-face class on the MA facilitated the participants' understanding of the sociocultural dimension (Little, 1995) of learner autonomy. In addition to this, two participants with little teaching experience emphasised that engaging with the global discussion forums inside the FutureLearn MOOC also strengthened their understanding of learner autonomy regarding the sociocultural dimension. They also mentioned how learning on the MOOC empowered them to take responsibility for their own learning process, as they could choose the steps to take. They viewed the MOOCs in terms of 'self-access learning' (Manning, Morrison, & McIlroy, 2014, p. 294) and declared that

4. Statement 13.8 of the survey in Table 1:
https://research-publishing.box.com/s/izradrzmmu5dd1ia2zueotanhv6f33c8

5. Statements 12.1-12.4 of the survey in Table 2:
https://research-publishing.box.com/s/izradrzmmu5dd1ia2zueotanhv6f33c8

6. Statements 14.1-14.6 of the survey in Tables 3 and 4:
https://research-publishing.box.com/s/izradrzmmu5dd1ia2zueotanhv6f33c8

through using it they had come to understand the conceptualisation of learner autonomy. However, the other two participants who were experienced teachers in China believed that it was the teacher's responsibility to select appropriate learning content for students when learning on the MOOC, because they believed that students might not be able to choose an appropriate learning course that benefitted them. Such a belief may root in the traditional teacher-centred educational cultures. For example, "students are used to high levels of personal support and assistance from their teachers, both in class and with assignments" (Cao, 2011, p. 4), because "teachers are considered wise, authority figures whose word has great weight' (McLaren, 1998, in Cao, 2011, p. 7).

3.3. Research question 3

Data collected from the VSR interviews were used to triangulate the results from both the surveys and the semi-structured interviews, and the initial findings suggested that there was a strong connection between the participants' perceptions of learner autonomy and their actual practice in promoting it. However, a gap was identified between some of the participants' theoretical beliefs and their microteaching practice. For instance, the participant with twelve-year teaching experience defined learner autonomy as "the teacher gives students enough freedom in their learning process", and "the students should take control of their learning and they should be leading their learning activities" (Participant 4, survey 18/11/2017). In addition to this, they also held a positive attitude towards fostering learner autonomy as mentioned in their semi-structured interview. However, when the microteaching video was analysed, it became apparent that they were not giving control over to their students in their teaching practice, instead they delivered a very tutor-centred session. Hence, while originally it was believed that they had grasped the concept of autonomy, it became clear that they had now and that they were stuck with the "liminal stage" (Land et al., 2005, p. 55) and instead of displaying understanding they demonstrated 'mimicry'. They could 'recite' the definition of the concept of learner autonomy, but they could not put it into practice. The ontological transformation of their beliefs had not taken place, they had not 'become' a teacher implementing autonomy, despite having stated that they believed they wanted to implement an autonomous approach. It was interesting to notice that the participants with fewer years of teaching experience were more willing to put their beliefs on learner autonomy in practice in their microteaching session.

4. Conclusion

The results of the current study revealed that integrating a FutureLearn MOOC into an existing MA course could promote the Chinese ELT students' understanding of the threshold concept of learner autonomy, especially for those participants who had little teaching experience. They also illustrated that engaging with an autonomy-supportive environment could foster learner autonomy, even if the learners are from traditional teacher-centred educational cultures. However, more experienced Chinese teachers appeared to be reluctant to embrace autonomy in their practice. For this reason, it is suggested that teacher educators should encourage trainee teachers to reflect on their prior learning or teaching experience and compare it with their current learning experience in order to help them identify any potential gaps that may hinder their understanding of learner autonomy. In addition to this, VSR is a viable technique which could be used to help trainee teachers or teacher educators to reflect on the alignment between their own teaching beliefs and their actual practice.

References

Armstrong, J. S. (2012). National learning in higher education. *Encyclopedia of Sciences of Learning*, 2426-2433.

Benson, P. (2006). Autonomy in language teaching and learning. *Language Teaching, 40*, 21-40. https://doi.org/10.1017/S0261444806003958

Cao, T. N. (2011). Impacts of socio-culture on the development of autonomous learning: a lens of Vietnamese context. *Journal of Studies in Education, 1*(1), 1-19.

Chang, H., & Holt, R. (1994). A Chinese perspective on face as inter-relational concern. In S. Ting-Toomey (Ed.), *The challenge of facework: cross-cultural and interpersonal issues* (pp. 95-132). SUNY Press.

Gieve, S., & Clark, R., (2005). The Chinese approach to learning: cultural trait or situated response? The case of a self-directed learning programme. *System*, 33(2), 261-276. https://doi.org/10.1016/j.system.2004.09.015

Jin, L., & Cortazzi, M. (1993). Cultural orientation and academic language use. In D. Graddol, L. Thompson, & M. Byram (Eds), *Language and culture* (pp. 84-97). Multilingual Matters.

Jin, L., & Cortazzi, M. (1996). This way is very different from Chinese ways. In: M. Hewings & T. Dudley-Evans (Eds), *Evaluation and course design in EAP* (pp. 205-216). Macmillan.

Land, R., Cousin, G., Meyer, J. H. F., & Davies, P. (2005). Threshold concepts and troublesome knowledge (3): implications for course design and evaluation. In C. Rust (Ed.), *Improving Student Learning*. Oxford Centre for Staff and Learning.

Little, D. (1995). Learning as dialogue: the dependence of learner autonomy on teacher autonomy. *System, 23*(2), 175-181. https://doi.org/10.1016/0346-251X(95)00006-6

Littlewood, W. (1999). Defining and developing autonomy in Eastern Asian context. *Applied Linguistics, 20*(1), 71-94. https://doi.org/10.1093/applin/20.1.71

Manning, C., Morrison, B. R., & McIlroy, T. (2014). MOOCs in language education and professional teacher development: possibilities and potential. *Studies in Self-Access Learning Journal, 5*(3), 294-308.

McLaren, M. (1998). *Interpreting culture differences*. Peter Francis publisher.

Meyer, J. H. F., & Land, R. (2003). Threshold concepts and troublesome knowledge: linkages to ways of thinking and practising within the disciplines. Occasional Report 4. http://www.etl.tla.ed.ac.uk/docs/ETLreport4.pdf

Meyer, J. H. F., & Land, R. (2006). *Overcoming barriers to student understanding threshold concepts and troublesome knowledge*. Routledge.

Orsini-Jones, M. (2015). *Innovative pedagogies series: integrating a MOOC into the MA in English language teaching at Coventry University. Innovation in blended learning practice*. Higher Education Academy. http://www.heacademy.ac.uk/system/files/marina_orsini_jones_final_1.pdf

Orsini-Jones, M., Conde Gafaro, B., & Altamimi, S. (2017). Integrating a MOOC into the postgraduate ELT curriculum: reflecting on students' beliefs with a MOOC blend. In Q. Kan & S. Bax (Eds), *Beyond the language classroom: researching MOOCs and other innovations* (pp. 71-83). Research-publishing.net. https://doi.org/10.14705/rpnet.2017.mooc2016.672

Wang, H. (2008). Learner autonomy and the Chinese context. *Journal of Asian Social Science, 4*(7), 114-120. https://doi.org/10.5539/ass.v4n7p114

6 OIL for English for business: the intercultural product pitch

Andrew Preshous[1], An Ostyn[2], and Nicole Keng[3]

Abstract

The Intercultural Product Pitch OIL (Online International Learning) Project set out to broaden the international experience for a small cohort of undergraduate students by enabling them to collaborate on a series of activities that would raise intercultural awareness and improve key communication skills. The project involved collaboration between International Business and Marketing students based in the UK and students from institutions in Belgium and Finland. This paper describes the key stages of this OIL project, highlighting how it can enhance students' global learning experience.

Keywords: online international learning, intercultural competence, virtual mobility, virtual learning environment.

1.   Introduction

Internationalising the curriculum has become a key objective in Higher Education (HE) in the UK with many institutions in recent years focusing on different strategies to "prepare graduates to live in and contribute responsibly to a globally interconnected society" (Higher Education Academy, 2016, n.p.).

1. Coventry University, Coventry, United Kingdom; andrew.preshous@coventry.ac.uk

2. VIVES University College, Kortrijk, Belgium; an.ostyn@vives.be

3. Vaasa University, Vaasa, Finland; nicole.keng@uva.fi

How to cite this chapter: Preshous, A., Ostyn, A., & Keng, N. (2018). OIL for English for business: the intercultural product pitch. In M. Orsini-Jones & S. Smith (Eds), *Flipping the blend through MOOCs, MALL and OIL – new directions in CALL* (pp. 41-50). Research-publishing.net. https://doi.org/10.14705/rpnet.2018.23.789

A crucial component of the internationalisation agenda in HE is the development of intercultural competence as defined by a group of intercultural scholars in the Delphi study (Deardorff, 2004, cited in Deardorff, 2006) as: "the ability to communicate effectively and appropriately in intercultural situations based on one's intercultural knowledge, skills, and attitudes" (pp. 247-248).

Increasing student mobility to develop intercultural awareness is recognised as a core element of internationalisation strategy, but it is not always possible for large numbers of students to travel abroad. Therefore, creating opportunities for learners to engage in online communication with their peers in different parts of the world has become more commonplace. The benefits of OIL projects are outlined by Villar and Rajpal (2016): "[v]irtual mobility initiatives such as OIL are one of the most flexible, versatile and inclusive approaches in the provision of experiential learning opportunities aimed at facilitating students' intercultural competence development" (p. 81).

Many recent studies have pointed out other positive features that collaborative online learning can offer. Marcillo-Gomez and Desilus (2016) placed an emphasis on the "unique experience" (p. 34) that Mexican and American students took from an online collaboration focusing on the similarities and differences in their cultures. In the student-driven MexCo Project (Orsini-Jones et al., 2015), it was noted that the Mexican and British participants created "a sense of ownership in the knowledge-sharing process" (p. 225).

It has been pointed out, however, that initiating and offering virtual exchanges is not always a straightforward process. O'Dowd (2013) investigated the extent to which barriers to the integration of telecollaboration in HE still exist and found that the most significant obstacles were the time needed to set up and run exchanges and the problems encountered with assessment in relation to institutional requirements. Some strategies were put forward on how to overcome these obstacles, such as building reliable partnerships and adapting to the local institution's needs. Other studies by Stier (2006) and Castro, Woodlin, Lundgren, and Byram (2016) have focused on the wider dimensions of internationalisation and student mobility.

Even though there are challenges when setting up and running virtual mobility exchanges, this paper aims to illustrate how OIL projects can offer rewarding outcomes through careful planning, focused objectives, and collaboration.

2.   Method

The overall framework was based on three basic requirements for OIL projects set out by Villar and Rajpal (2016) and summarised below:

- Students engage with international peers on discipline-related content.

- Collaborative activities must have internationalised learning outcomes.

- There must be a reflective component based on the intercultural interaction.

In this OIL project, Malaysian, Chinese, and Indonesian International Business students in the UK established links with their Belgian or Finnish peers online using a tailor-made Moodle platform, then delivered a product pitch presentation before responding to another group's output. Cooperating with their peers in other countries on this collaborative online project would broaden these students' international experiences and aimed to address the research questions specified below:

- How can online international exchanges develop and raise intercultural awareness?

- What key communication skills for the workplace can be enhanced by online international exchanges?

Participation in the process would also provide useful opportunities for critical reflection and enhance individual employability profiles.

The different stages and participant tasks of the OIL project are outlined below:

Stage 1: Establish contact
- Build relationship/find out about different cultural contexts

Stage 2: Task: online simulation scenario
- Pitch a product/service from your country to a new global market

Stage 3: Feedback
- Respond to other presentations
- Feedback provided by subject experts

Stage 4: Reflection
- Reflect on feedback and experience

More details on each stage will be provided in the following section.

3.   Results and discussion

The participants communicated via Open Moodle, a Virtual Learning Environment (VLE), or OneDrive (used in the second iteration), platforms which allow students to post questions and comments as well as being a repository for the video presentations. In the first stage of the project, the students introduced themselves by creating and uploading presentations about their courses, learning contexts, and interests. This generated initial interactions containing a variety of cultural content, for example:

Finnish student (Fs): "Can you tell us something about student free time activities in Malaysia?".

Malaysian student (Ms): "In my city Kuala Lumpur, local students' free time is usually spent hanging out in mamak stalls (a 24 hour restaurant) where the foods are cheap... What local Finnish dishes would you recommend to foreigners?".

(Fs): "My favourite Finnish food is 'rye bread' or a candy called 'salmiakk'".

In the second version of the project, students used Skype™, giving a synchronous and more natural element to the interaction illustrated by the exchange below:

Belgian student (Bs): "Can you give us a rare fact about your home country?".

Indonesian student (Is): Probably our traffic jams... it's really bad so if you come to our country you'll be like, what's going on, it's traffic jams everywhere... and also we have lots of islands... maybe thousands, if you know Bali..?".

Bs: "Have you been to Bali?".

Is: "Yeah... numerous times".

Bs: "I'm jealous [laughter]".

The main communicative task in this OIL project involved the students pitching a product from their own country to a new global market, allowing them to draw on their own culture but also encouraging research into a different cultural context. This task would add a different dimension to the students' learning experience as it would help prepare them for professional contexts via activities involving meaningful, practical engagement. This echoes the sentiments voiced by Evans (2013) and "the need for a simulation-based approach" (p. 291), as suggested in his study of task design for workplace communication.

For the OIL task, the Malaysian cohort pitched a tea product to the Finnish group who decided to promote a lunchtime dining service. The Chinese group launched a traditional body treatment product ('fire cupping') on the Belgian market, whilst the Belgian students put forward a launderette-café specifically targeting Chinese students. After conversing with their peers, the Indonesian students noted that "it seems most of students in Belgium study hard and party hard...", and decided to pitch a herbal remedy for hangovers and other ailments.

The pitches were varied in format – some were standard PowerPoint presentations, others incorporated humorous and creative visual elements. After uploading the presentations to the VLE, the students responded to the pitches which resulted in some interesting interactions. For instance, it was pointed out to the Belgians that promotion via well-known social media sites would not be possible in China due to restricted internet access. Other exchanges demonstrated constructive intercultural communication, as in the response to the fire cupping pitch:

> Bs: "Perhaps there is an extra product you could sell (like an additional oil treatment) to rehydrate the skin? This solution could end up increasing profits".

> Chinese student (Cs): "We found your advice very thoughtful. We think it would be great to cooperate with skin care brand to promote new product bundles".

Another group responded favourably to the herbal remedy pitch by the Indonesian group as they felt it filled a gap in the market:

> Bs: "This original product does not exist in Belgium yet... and we think this could be very popular with students".

A distinctive feature of the project was that feedback on the pitches was provided by tutors with expertise in different areas – cultural, business, and language/ delivery. It was felt that insights from three perspectives would be beneficial for the students. Sample comments are shown below:

Intercultural: "Particularly impressive was the research you did on tea products in Finland which shows a higher understanding of why intercultural awareness is a key quality in business pitching".

Business/marketing: "The target market that you suggested is rather broad and only defined in terms of demographic characteristics".

Language/delivery: "Consider other ways to engage the audience in a pitch, e.g. product 'demo', alternatives to the 'traditional' PPT presentation".

4.   Evaluation and outcomes

Qualitative data on the participants' reflections on the OIL project was collected using questionnaires, online forums, and semi-structured interviews. Staff co-ordinators' evaluations of their students' involvement and the benefits of the project were also gathered. Many comments indicated that participants felt that business communication skills had been advanced and the project was perceived to have a relevance to future employment:

Ms: "The most useful part in this project is presentation... because it helps me to improve confidence in a professional context which I will face in my further career".

The target of raising intercultural awareness was emphasised and some of the unique elements offered by the project were also highlighted:

Bs: "It provided an exclusive opportunity for us to interact with students from another country and cultural background. It definitely raised my cultural awareness and the differences between others".

Feedback from the different partner coordinators also illustrated a range of positive elements in the exchanges:

"Giving them the insight that language-learning is effective and satisfying once you can apply the skill in real life".

"This online contact makes the learners more conscious than just reading and studying about cultural differences".

"The project topic itself required them [Finnish students] to think with a more global view and to communicate with other students online, which allowed them to interact without feeling embarrassed".

"Presenting a strong domestic product or service and thus increasing some pride of a community/company you are part of".

The feedback given by staff and student participants emphasises that the OIL project offers many opportunities and benefits, meeting key individual and institutional requirements, as summarised below:

- Interaction with peers from other countries to raise intercultural awareness.

- Integration of business/marketing knowledge and English language skills.

- Development of key communication skills, teamwork, and critical reflection.

- Engagement in digitalised learning: video editing and online exchanges.

- Enhancement of employability profiles.

Collaborations involving different international partners and contexts do present challenges in terms of timings and staging (holidays and exam periods, for example), so developing a more closely structured timescale is an area to work on. The use of an intercultural sensitivity scale (pre-/post-project) would allow a more systematic analysis of key data. It is also important to keep up with fast-moving advances in technology and worth considering the latest digital platforms and digital indicators of accomplishment, such as Open Badges. There are also plans to enlarge the scale of the OIL project to incorporate a wider global and cultural span.

5. Conclusions

Although there are considerable challenges and complexities in setting up and implementing virtual mobility collaborations, the positive feedback on this OIL project clearly supports the development of an innovative internationalised curriculum that allows students to engage in digitalised learning in order to improve business communication skills and enhance intercultural competence.

Acknowledgements

The authors would like to thank the three institutions involved, Coventry University, Vives College, and the University of Vaasa for their support as well as all the students who have participated so enthusiastically in this OIL project. Andrew, the Project Lead, would also like to thank the Centre for Global Engagement at Coventry University for their backing and the valuable help and advice provided by Dr Marina Orsini-Jones.

References

Castro, P., Woodlin, J., Lundgren, U., & Byram, M. (2016). Student mobility and internationalisation in higher education: perspectives from practitioners. *Language and Intercultural Communication, 16*(3), 418-436. https://doi.org/10.1080/14708477.2016.1168052

Deardorff, D. K. (2004). *The identification and assessment of intercultural competence as a student outcome of international education at institutions of higher education in the United States.* Unpublished dissertation, North Carolina State University, Raleigh. https://repository.lib.ncsu.edu/handle/1840.16/5733

Deardorff, D. K. (2006). Identification and assessment of intercultural competence as a student outcome of internationalization. *Journal of Studies in International education, 10*(3), 241-266. https://doi.org/10.1177/1028315306287002

Evans, S. (2013). Designing tasks for the business English classroom. *ELT Journal, 67*(3), 281-293. https://doi.org/10.1093/elt/cct013

Higher Education Academy. (2016). Framework for internationalising higher education https://www.heacademy.ac.uk/enhancement/frameworks/framework-internationalising-higher-education

Marcillo-Gomez, M., & Desilus, B. (2016). Collaborative online international learning experience in practice: opportunities and challenges. *Journal of Technology Management & Innovation, 11*(1), 30-35. https://doi.org/10.4067/S0718-27242016000100005

O'Dowd, R. (2013). Telecollaborative networks in university higher education: overcoming barriers to integration. *Internet and Higher Education, 18*, 47-53. https://doi.org/10.1016/j.iheduc.2013.02.001

Orsini-Jones, M., Lloyd, E., Gazeley, Z., Lopez-Vera, B., & Bescond, G. (2015). Student-driven intercultural awareness raising with MexCo: agency, autonomy and threshold concepts in a telecollaborative project between the UK and Mexico. In N. Tcherepashenets (Ed.), *Globalizing on-line: telecollaboration, internationalization and social justice* (pp. 199-239). Peter Lang.

Stier, J. (2006). Internationalisation, intercultural communication and intercultural competence. *Journal of Intercultural Communication, 11*, 1-11.

Villar, D., & Rajpal, B. (2016). Online international learning. *Perspectives: Policy and Practice in Higher Education, 20*(2-3), 75-82.

7 A role-reversal model of telecollaborative practice: the student-driven and student-managed *FloCo*

Elwyn Lloyd[1], Abraham Cerveró-Carrascosa[2], and Courtney Green[3]

Abstract

This paper, based both on a talk given at the BMELTT symposium in June 2017 and one given at the UNICollaboration conference held in Krakow in April 2018, reports on *FloCo* (Florida Universitària/ Coventry University), a telecollaborative project where the roles of teacher and student were reversed. A student from Coventry University (CU), studying on a Bachelor of Arts Honours in English and TEFL (Teaching English as a Foreign Language), obtained a third year placement to teach English in Spain at Florida Universitària (FU) in València. The student had taken part in the online intercultural exchange *MexCo*, between Coventry and Mexico, in her first year at university, and decided to set up a similar exchange between the class of students she was teaching in Spain and Year 1 students on Spanish degrees at CU. The shared 'expert student'/staff reflections on the project are reported here and compared with the outcomes of related online intercultural exchanges (e.g. *MexCo* and *CoCo*).

Keywords: *FloCo*, *MexCo*, role-reversal, telecollaboration, Coventry University, Florida Universitària.

1. Coventry University, Coventry, United Kingdom; e.lloyd@coventry.ac.uk

2. Florida Universitària, València, Spain; acervero@florida-uni.es

3. Coventry University, Coventry, United Kingdom; greenc21@uni.coventry.ac.uk

How to cite this chapter: Lloyd. E., Cerveró-Carrascosa, A., & Green, C. (2018). A role-reversal model of telecollaborative practice: the student-driven and student-managed *FloCo*. In M. Orsini-Jones & S. Smith (Eds), *Flipping the blend through MOOCs, MALL and OIL – new directions in CALL* (pp. 51-58). Research-publishing.net. https://doi.org/10.14705/rpnet.2018.23.790

1.   Introduction

CU staff in English and Languages have engaged in telecollaboration aimed at developing global citizenship skills for undergraduate students through Online International Learning (OIL) or Virtual Exchange (VE) since academic year 2011-2012. The OIL projects started with universities in Mexico (Universidad Nacional Autónoma de México and Universidad de Monterrey) and, since academic year 2016-2017, also involved telecollaboration with universities in Europe, such as the Université de Haute Alsace in France (*CoCo*, see Lloyd, 2017) and FU in Spain. Each of these exchanges has been following a similar format, modelled on successful telecollaborative work by Furstenberg and Levet at MIT (the *Cultura* project, see Furstenberg & Levet, 2010) and by Robert O'Dowd, based at the University of León in Spain (e.g. O'Dowd, 2007). Each project is supported by a tailor-made Moodle environment maintained by Coventry University and includes a series of tasks that participating students carry out in blended learning mode: face-to-face in their respective home institutions and online, via synchronous and asynchronous exchanges, with the international partners they are working with (Orsini-Jones & Lee, 2018).

All students communicate mainly via Moodle, but also utilise Skype, email, Facebook, and other e-platforms of their choice outside Moodle. The reason why Moodle is kept as the official e-platform for these exchanges has to do with the data protection laws in Europe and the ethical clearance issues relating to the telecollaborative projects if staff want to carry out research on them. As Moodle is a proprietary platform that can be adapted to comply with EU legislation, staff engaging with *FloCo* decided to carry on using it, even if this virtual learning environment does not offer as many Web 2.0 affordances as other e-tools.

The tasks, that are co-designed with the OIL partners and the students involved in the exchange, aim to adhere to the principles for intercultural language learning and teaching outlined by Liddicoat and Scarino (2013, pp. 57-59, cited in Orsini-Jones, 2015, p. 52). They are grounded and experiential and comprise the following elements: active construction; making connections;

social interaction; and reflection and responsibility. The key features of OIL at Coventry University[4] are that:

- it involves a cross-border collaboration or interaction with people from different backgrounds and cultures;

- students must engage in some sort of online interaction, whether it is asynchronous or synchronous;

- it must be driven by a set of internationalised learning outcomes aimed at developing global perspectives and/or fostering students' intercultural competences; and

- there must be a reflective component that helps students think critically about such interaction.

Despite the fact that the two higher education institutions involved in *FloCo* are quite different (CU has around 28,000 students and is a state university, while FU is a small private university with around 4,000 students), both share the drive to engage in OIL to support their students in developing global citizenship skills. This also includes teaching and assessing intercultural competence, as discussed by Deardorff (2011).

The main aims of *FloCo* are:

- to develop an international intercultural exchange between students of Spanish at CU and FU pre-service TEFL teachers;

- to enhance the intercultural awareness and communicative competence of all participants; and

---

4. Centre for Global Engagement, CU, 2018, internal document.

- to provide students and teachers with an opportunity for virtual international mobility and to enhance digital fluency.

In its first occurrence, in academic year 2017-2018, *FloCo* ran for five weeks in the first semester (Nov-Dec).

At CU, *FloCo* is embedded in the module *Introduction to Studying English and Languages at University* (its credit value being 5 out of the 60 ECTS credits for the year), a module taken by all students studying on Single and Joint Honours Degrees in English and Languages. The module aims to prepare students for university study and the following are covered in it: academic writing; group project work; digital and presentation skills; and intercultural awareness competences development and practice. The tasks linked to *FloCo* make up 50% of the module mark (2.5 ECTS). Students carry out three tasks in collaboration with the partners (video introductions, *Cultura* tasks, and a group interview on a chosen topic to do with current affairs) and then they present the outcomes of the project as a group. This is followed by an individual reflective report on the exchange. The group presentation is worth 30% of the total module mark and the individual written reflection 20%. Both tasks must include information gathered through the OIL collaborative activities.

At FU, *FloCo* is embedded into *English Language II* (6 ECTS), a module in the final year of a four-year degree in primary education; it is a module aimed at improving the English proficiency of the FU students who must have a B2 CEFR (Common European Framework of Reference for languages) level or equivalent in a foreign language to qualify as primary school teachers. The assessment of the *FloCo* activities – which count for 15% of the module mark – is as follows: 60% for the introductions video, 15% for the *Cultura* tasks, 15% for the interviews, and 10% self and peer assessment (reflective).

All students have access to online materials on intercultural-awareness raising, such as lectures/vidcasts on intercultural awareness topics and global citizenship, developing intercultural communicative competence and 'cyberpragmatic competence' (Yus Ramos, 2011). All students complete the word associations, sentence completions, 'reactions to situations' surveys, and quizzes adapted from the MIT *Cultura* suite (Furstenberg & Levet, 2010), and all students engage in asynchronous discussion forums where they comment on each other's introduction videos and responses on the *Cultura* tasks. Fourteen students took part in this exchange from FU and seventeen from CU. The students were 'matched' in groups of 4-5 in each country.

2.   A role-reversal telecollaborative model

Although 'expert students' had been involved in the delivery and managing of *MexCo* (Orsini-Jones et al., 2015) and *CoCo* (Orsini-Jones & Lee, 2018) that both preceded *FloCo*, in *FloCo* there was an interesting student-centred 'turn'. A CU student who had taken part in *MexCo* in her first year at CU obtained a work placement at FU to shadow English teachers there as a language assistant. Working in collaboration with her English and TEFL tutor based at CU, and her mentor at FU, she set up and managed *FloCo* from Spain. This made Courtney Green, the student who managed *FloCo* and one of the authors of this paper, the main intercultural mediator for the project (Deardorff, 2006). Courtney helped staff see the VE through her eyes, in a role-reversal model previously explored at CU, where an 'expert student' helps staff to explore troublesome areas of knowledge and understanding through her view of said areas while helping her peers and/or 'mentees' (see Orsini-Jones, 2014; Orsini-Jones, 2015, pp. 47-48 on this point).

Intercultural communicative competence has already been identified as a 'threshold concept' (Orsini-Jones, 2015; Orsini-Jones & Lee, 2018), that is to say a concept that challenges students' worldview:

> "A threshold concept can be considered as akin to a portal, opening up a new and previously inaccessible way of thinking about something. It represents a transformed way of understanding, or interpreting, or viewing something without which the learner cannot progress. As a consequence of comprehending a threshold concept there may thus be a

transformed internal view of subject matter, subject landscape, or even world view" (Meyer & Land, 2003, p. 3).

The mediation of the OIL project by an expert student appeared to facilitate its adoption by CU students who had previously resisted 'buying into' the ethos of similar projects. The CU tutor involved also found that he had to deal with fewer problems arising from the project than in previous years, and observed that students were more at ease with the tasks than they had been in *MexCo* and *CoCo*.

The reflective reports demonstrated that students were grasping difficult concepts relating to intercultural awareness and were developing the Intecultural Communicative Competence skills highlighted by Helm and Guth (2010), which include "Critical Cultural Awareness", together with "New Online Literacies", such as "Computer literacy", "Information Literacy", and "New Media Literacy" (Helm & Guth, 2010, p. 74).

3.   Conclusion

By completing *FloCo*, students have opportunities to familiarise themselves with, acquire knowledge of, and research into concepts relating to – and also leading to – the development of intercultural competence, which is essential for success in foreign language learning.

Student feedback confirms that *FloCo* was beneficial for the students who participated in that it allowed them to develop the aforementioned competences and required them to reflect on the 'direct evidences', as suggested by Deardorff (2011). A student who had the knowledge and skills to manage the project enabled tutors and students from both institutions to reflect on attitudes towards the target cultures and made the completion of the activities easier to manage. Moreover, the efficiency of the student-turned-tutor (Courtney) ensured that students who took part met their deadlines in almost all the activities at both ends.

Acknowledgements

We would like to thank all the students and staff who have participated in the *FloCo* and related projects to date.

References

Deardorff, D. K. (2006). The identification and assessment of intercultural competence. *Journal of Studies in International Education,* 10(3), 241-266. https://doi.org/10.1177/1028315306287002

Deardorff, D. K. (2011). Assessing intercultural competence. *New directions for institutional research, 149,* 65-79. https://doi.org/10.1002/ir.381

Furstenberg, G., & Levet, S. (2010). Integrating telecollaboration into the language classroom: some insights. In S. Guth & F. Helm (Eds), *Telecollaboration 2.0* (pp. 305-336). Peter Lang.

Helm, F., & Guth, S. (2010). The Multifarious Goals of Telecollaboration 2.0: theoretical and practical implications.In S. Guth & F. Helm (Eds), *Telecollaboration 2.0* (pp. 69-106). Peter Lang.

Liddicoat, A. J., & Scarino, A. (2013). *Intercultural language teaching and learning.* Wiley Blackwell. https://doi.org/10.1002/9781118482070

Lloyd, E. (2017). Developing global graduate competencies through an OIL project – *CoCo* (Coventry-Colmar). Talk given at the BMELTT Symposium held at Coventry University 29-30 June. https://youtu.be/jtshJGKk4x8

Meyer, J. H. F., & Land, R. (2003). Threshold concepts and troublesome knowledge: linkages to ways of thinking and practising within the disciplines - Occasional Report 4. http://www.tla.ed.ac.uk/etl/docs/ETLreport4.pdf

O'Dowd, R. (Ed.). (2007). *Online intercultural exchange: an introduction for foreign language teachers.* Multilingual Matters.

Orsini-Jones, M. (2014). Towards a role-reversal model of threshold concept pedagogy. In C. O'Mahony, A. Buchanan, M. O'Rourke, & B. Higgs (Eds), *Threshold concepts: from personal practice to communities of practice* (pp 78-82). Proceedings of the National Academy's Sixth Annual Conference and the Fourth Biennial Threshold Concepts Conference [e-publication]. NAIRTL. http://www.nairtl.ie/documents/EPub_2012Proceedings.pdf#page=88

Orsini-Jones, M. (2015). A reflective e-learning journey from the dawn of CALL to web 2.0 intercultural communicative competence (ICC). In K. Borthwick, E. Corradini, & A. Dickens (Eds), *10 years of the LLAS elearning symposium: case studies in good practice* (pp. 43-56). Research-publishing.net. https://doi.org/10.14705/rpnet.2015.000266

Orsini-Jones, M., & Lee, F. (2018). *Intercultural communicative competence for global citizenship: identifying rules of engagement in telecollaboration.* Palgrave MacMillan. https://doi.org/10.1057/978-1-137-58103-7

Orsini-Jones, M., Lloyd, E., Gazeley, Z., Lopez-Vera, B., & Bescond, G. (2015). Student-driven intercultural awareness raising with MexCo: agency, autonomy and threshold concepts in a telecollaborative project between the UK and Mexico. In N. Tcherepashenets (Ed.), *Globalizing on-line: telecollaboration, internationalization and social justice* (pp. 199-239). Peter Lang.

Yus Ramos, F. (2011). *Cyberpragmatics: internet-mediated communication in context.* John Benjamins.

8 Chinese segmentation and collocation: a platform for blended learning

Simon Smith[1]

Abstract

Mandarin Chinese is an increasingly popular world language and object of study, and while there are numerous online character learning apps and flashcard systems, very little research has been done on inductive or autonomous learning in the realm of collocation acquisition. I propose a new Chinese implementation of a trusted corpus-based platform, currently available for English and several other languages, accompanied and enhanced by an adaptive approach to Chinese segmentation approach, whereby different ways of carving up a given sentence are selectively displayed to the learner.

Keywords: Chinese, Mandarin, CALL, blended learning, segmentation.

1. Introduction and background

Mandarin Chinese has the largest number of native speakers of all languages (Simons & Fennig, 2018). More and more people are starting to learn Chinese, in the UK and globally. Centres of Chinese cultural exchange, such as Confucius Institutes, are opening up, and increasing numbers of universities, and more recently schools as well, are starting to offer Mandarin Chinese programmes. It is fast becoming a global language, and more tools and resources enabling its learning are needed. Lo (2016), for example, shows that heritage Chinese students from the UK who are native speakers of English and Cantonese find

1. Coventry University, Coventry, United Kingdom; simon.smith@coventry.ac.uk

How to cite this chapter: Smith, S. (2018). Chinese segmentation and collocation: a platform for blended learning. In M. Orsini-Jones & S. Smith (Eds), *Flipping the blend through MOOCs, MALL and OIL – new directions in CALL* (pp. 59-65). Research-publishing.net. https://doi.org/10.14705/rpnet.2018.23.791

the mastery of Mandarin important for their careers. A renewed commitment to trade partnership with China has been noted by the UK government (Gibb & Johnson, 2015), and one likely impact of Brexit is that increased trade with China will turn command of Chinese into a yet more marketable skill.

Mandarin Chinese is popular among students of all ages, and Chen (2014) reports success in teaching the language at primary school in Britain. Secondary school uptake has increased in recent years, with General Certificate of Secondary Education (GCSE) entries up 18% in 2015, despite an overall decline in pupils sitting language exams (Guardian, 2015). Jin (2014) discusses the opportunities for enhancing students' intercultural competencies that the learning of Mandarin Chinese affords.

Modern approaches to language learning, especially English learning, emphasise the use of authentic texts (Gilmore, 2007; Nunan, 1999), so that vocabulary and patterns may be acquired by learners in genuine contexts. Such authentic texts may be conveniently gathered together in a *corpus* – that is to say, a 'body of texts', defined more explicitly by McEnery, Xiao, and Tono (2006) as "a collection of (1) *machine-readable* (2) *authentic* texts [...] which is (3) *sampled* to be (4) *representative* of a particular language or language variety" (their emphasis, p. 5). The potential of *inductive* (as opposed to *deductive*) learning, where learners look at data to try to establish systematic rules, rather than being taught the rules explicitly, is now widely accepted in educational circles (Dörnyei, 2014; Larsen-Freeman & Long, 2014). Johns (1991) made what was then an innovative use of inductive learning, in an approach named Data-Driven Learning (DDL), which entails getting students to consult corpora directly. With DDL, learners can search for particular lexical and grammatical patterns that interest them. They can be trained to adopt an inductive or discovery-based approach to learning, where they work out a grammatical rule or pattern of usage from a plethora of authentic examples, as opposed to a deductive and more traditional approach where the teacher lays out rules, words, and patterns and gets the learner to practise them. There has been increasing interest in DDL in language teaching circles over the years, and the approach lends itself well to blended learning, which by definition involves autonomous study.

Almost all this work has so far focused on English learning; although Chinese is widely spoken and studied, and while there is no shortage of flashcard apps and character-practice software, there have been very few attempts to harness the power of the corpus for this language. One particularly powerful corpus-based tool, currently available for English and several other languages, is Sketch Engine for Language Learning (SkELL) (Baisa & Suchomel, 2014).

On SkELL, Chinese students can obtain three kinds of output displays about the usage of words, derived from large corpora. The first display is Example Sentences, which finds the most salient dictionary-like examples from the corpus. Then there is Word Sketch, which offers a one-page synopsis of the usage of a word, indicating for example which collocations it is most associated with, and what the grammatical relations are (e.g. what is the most salient object of this verb, or most salient modifier of this noun). The third display type is called Similar Words, a distributional thesaurus. SkELL is powered by the Sketch Engine (SkE; Baisa & Suchomel, 2014), a corpus query software suite which does not specifically target language learners, but which does allow access to a number of large Chinese corpora. Most of these have been segmented (broken up into words) and POS-tagged (Smith, 2017).

2.   Methodology and approach

In this work, SkELL is extended to the Chinese language, allowing learners to view vocabulary in authentic collocational contexts, presenting a variety of example sentences, and showing how words participate in collocations and interact grammatically with other words. The implementation incorporates a standalone adaptive segmentation system using Hidden Markov Model (HMM) technology, and it will be evaluated using the training and test corpora of the first Chinese Segmentation Bakeoff of the Association for Computational Linguistics Chinese special interest group (Sproat & Emerson, 2003). A learner-friendly interface will be designed, and its use piloted with a group of intermediate Chinese learners who will be asked to evaluate its usefulness (in particular its adaptive features). The study will experiment with different ways of presenting the varying granularity of segmentation to the learner, aiming to provide for ease of use in a blended learning context.

A particular challenge for learners of Chinese, an addition to the obvious complexity of the characters themselves, is the identification of word boundaries. The Chinese SkELL implementation will therefore incorporate a new adaptive segmentation system, which is described below.

3. Chinese vocabulary and segmentation

In the absence of clear orthographic information about word boundaries, as is available in English writing, it can be quite difficult to get even human informants to agree on where the word boundaries are in a Chinese sentence. It follows from that that it is quite difficult to write segmentation software to do the same task.

Early segmentation algorithms consisted of a dictionary search module supplemented by heuristics, typically a longest match (or maximum match) procedure (Deng & Long, 1987). This means that if several different ways of segmenting the sentence are potentially available, the way which includes the longest words will be selected.

The next phase of segmentation algorithms made use of statistical information: notably Mutual Information (MI) scores in the work of Sproat and Shih (1990), and Sun, Shen, and Tsou (1998), without the use of dictionaries. The segmenter currently in use by Baidu, the main Chinese search engine, exploits HMM technology, and offers the user of their so-called 'Jieba' segmentation software the option of adding in their own custom dictionary (Lin, 2015).

This study confronts and exploits the 'wordhood' challenge. It offers an adaptive segmentation approach, where different ways of carving up a given sentence are selectively displayed to the learner.

Wu (2003, p. 3) demonstrates how such an approach can benefit the different applications of Chinese Natural Language Processing (NLP): Machine Translation (MT), for example, generally needs the longest strings that are available in the bilingual lexicon being used, so a maximum matching algorithm is the most useful. For information retrieval, on the other hand, a user (such as a search engine user) might be interested in webpages that contain substrings of the string they entered, so a fine-grained segmentation might be more appropriate. I believe that, just as the varying granularities can be applied to different NLP applications, so too they can usefully address different language learning purposes in DDL.

For example, the string 中华人民共和国 is the official title of the People's Republic of China. This could be treated as one word, or segmented into two (中华人民 / 共和国) or three words (中华/人民/共和国). Alternatively, the learner is likely to be interested in the individual characters as morphemes, and finding out what other characters they pattern with. In a blended learning context, where guidance from the teacher is not always at hand, the student will be able to set the parameters for his or her own learning.

4. Conclusion and next steps

It was noted above that making different segmentation granularities available could benefit learners of Chinese. The adaptive segmenter described by Wu (2003) and Gao, Li, Wu, and Huang (2005) allows for several different levels of segmentation, within a "single annotated corpus that can be conveniently customised to meet different segmentation requirements" (Wu, 2003, p. 2).

Gao et al. (2005), with Wu as a co-author, implemented a similar system called MSRseg (Microsoft Research Segmenter), using transformation based learning (Brill, 1995). This is still available as a free download from Microsoft Research (although minus the adaptive component which is of particular relevance to this work). Gao et al. (2005) note that in actuality they retain only the segmentation that involves the smallest number of words, because "we currently do not know any effective way of using multiple segmentations in [NLP] applications" (p. 541).

Adaptive segmentation does not appear to have been revisited in the literature since, and there has not been any attempt that I am aware of to integrate such a segmentation model into language learning. I therefore consider our proposal to be innovative, practical, and timely.

References

Baisa, V., & Suchomel, V. (2014). SkELL – Web interface for English language learning. In *Eighth Workshop on Recent Advances in Slavonic Natural Language Processing* (pp. 63-70). Tribun EU.

Brill, E. (1995). Transformation-based error-driven learning and natural language processing: a case study in part-of-speech tagging. *Computational Linguistics, 21*(4), 543-565.

Chen, T. (2014). Teaching Chinese as a foreign language at primary school in England. *Quarterly Journal of Chinese Studies, 2*(4), 67-83.

Deng, Q., & Long, Z. (1987). A microcomputer retrieval system realising automatic information indexing in Chinese. *Journal of Information Science, 6*, 427-432 (in Chinese).

Dörnyei, Z. (2014). *The psychology of the language learner: individual differences in second language acquisition.* Routledge.

Gao, J., Li, M., Wu, A., & Huang, C. N. (2005). Chinese word segmentation and named entity recognition: a pragmatic approach. *Computational Linguistics, 31*(4), 531-574. https://doi.org/10.1162/089120105775299177

Gibb, N., & Johnson, J. (2015). *Press release: UK-China education partnership reaches new heights.* Department for Business, Innovation & Skills https://www.gov.uk/government/news/uk-china-education-partnership-reaches-new-heights

Gilmore, A. (2007). Authentic materials and authenticity in foreign language learning. *Language Teaching, 40*, 97-118. https://doi.org/10.1017/S0261444807004144

Guardian. (2015). *GCSE results: fall in numbers taking foreign languages 'a cause for concern'.* https://www.theguardian.com/education/2015/aug/20/gcse-results-fall-numbers-foreign-languages

Jin, T. (2014). Getting to know you: the development of intercultural competence as an essential element in learning Mandarin. *London Review of Education, 12*(1), 20-33. https://doi.org/10.18546/LRE.12.1.04

Johns, T. (1991). Should you be persuaded: two examples of data-driven learning. In T. Johns & P. King (Eds), *Classroom concordancing* (pp. 1-16). English Language Research.

Larsen-Freeman, D., & Long, M. H. (2014). *An introduction to second language acquisition research*. Routledge.

Lin, F. (2015). JIEBA 結巴中文斷詞. https://speakerdeck.com/fukuball/jieba-jie-ba-zhong-wen-duan-ci

Lo, L. (2016). Challenges faced by Cantonese speakers in a UK university Mandarin course. In C. Goria, O. Speicher, & S. Stollhans (Eds), *Innovative language teaching and learning at university: enhancing participation and collaboration* (pp. 139-145). Research-publishing.net. https://doi.org/10.14705/rpnet.2016.000415

McEnery, T., Xiao, R., & Tono, Y. (2006). *Corpus-based language studies: an advanced resource book*. Routledge

Nunan, D. (1999). *Second language teaching and learning*. Heinle & Heinle.

Simons, G., & Fennig, C. (Eds). (2018). *Ethnologue: languages of the world*. SIL International. http://www.ethnologue.com

Smith, S. (2017). SkELL: A discovery-based Chinese learning platform. In *Corpus Linguistics International Conference Abstracts*. http://paulslals.org.uk/ccr/CL2017ExtendedAbstracts.pdf

Sproat, R., & Emerson, T. (2003). The first international Chinese word segmentation bakeoff. In *Proceedings of the Second SIGHAN Workshop on Chinese Language Processing* (pp. 133-143). SIGHAN. https://doi.org/10.3115/1119250.1119269

Sproat, R., & Shih, C. (1990). A statistical method for finding word boundaries in Chinese text. *Computer Processing of Chinese and Oriental Languages, 4*(4), 336-51.

Sun, M., Shen, D., & Tsou, B. K. (1998). Chinese word segmentation without using lexicon and hand-crafted training data. In *Proceedings of the 17th international conference on Computational linguistics – Volume 2* (pp. 1265-1271). Association for Computational Linguistics.

Wu, A. (2003). Customizable segmentation of morphologically derived words in Chinese. *International Journal of Computational Linguistics and Chinese Language Processing, 8*(1), 1-27.

9 Student-teachers' beliefs concerning the usability of digital flashcards in ELT

Marwa Alnajjar[1] and Billy Brick[2]

Abstract

This paper reports on a study that explored five student-teachers' beliefs regarding the usability of three digital flashcard websites that can be used in a blended learning approach in English Language Teaching (ELT) classrooms. These student-teachers, who had previous teaching experience, were students on a year-long Master of Arts (MA) programme at Coventry University. Adopting a mixed-method research design, this study incorporated aspects of both surveys and case studies to explore different variables that could have an effect on the use of digital flashcards in blended learning classrooms. The websites' design features appeared to create two extreme reactions in student-teachers, suggesting it might be a significant factor in shaping their beliefs.

Keywords: blended learning, digital flashcards, vocabulary, CAVL, usability.

1. Introduction

Vocabulary learning, both incidental or deliberate (Nation, 2013), is pivotal to mastering a second language (Schmitt, 2008). However, direct deliberate vocabulary learning is more effective than incidental learning with regard to the quantity of acquired words and learning duration (Nation, 2013). Several

1. Royal College of Surgeons in Ireland - Medical University of Bahrain, Muharraq, Kingdom of Bahrain; marwa.alnajjar@gmail.com

2. Coventry University, Coventry, United Kingdom; lsx133@coventry.ac.uk

How to cite this chapter: Alnajjar, M., & Brick, B. (2018). Student-teachers' beliefs concerning the usability of digital flashcards in ELT. In M. Orsini-Jones & S. Smith (Eds), *Flipping the blend through MOOCs, MALL and OIL – new directions in CALL* (pp. 67-74). Research-publishing.net. https://doi.org/10.14705/rpnet.2018.23.792

experts, including Nation (2013) and Nakata (2011), recommend utilising flashcards, physical or digital, in deliberate vocabulary learning. One way to create digital flashcards includes using Computer-Assisted Vocabulary Learning (CAVL) tools, particularly websites, such as *Cram, Quizlet,* and *StudyStack.*

This study investigated the following questions:

- What are student-teachers' beliefs concerning the usability of *Cram, Quizlet,* and *StudyStack?*

- What variables shape student-teachers' beliefs?

- Will student-teachers incorporate digital flashcards in their classroom practice?

2.   Method

Following Dörnyei's (2007) quan→QUAL model of mixed-method research, data was collected using a survey, which combined Likert-scale statements and open-ended questions, and a focus group discussion. Student-teachers studying on the MA in ELT at Coventry University were selected using purposive sampling (see Table 1). In order to be able to determine a CAVL tool's usability, participants need to have basic knowledge of Computer-Assisted Language Learning (CALL) and of materials design. Thus, only student-teachers who completed the following two modules on the MA were selected: *CALL: Past, Present, and Future* and *Designing Language Training Materials.*

The MA students were asked to give feedback on their beliefs regarding the usability of Cram (2015), Quizlet (2015), and StudyStack (2015). These three websites are freemium and dedicated to creating digital flashcards. Users can share the flashcard sets they have created or access pre-existing sets created by others. Users can look for pre-existing sets concerning numerous topics using the search bar. The websites also have other features for further practice with the vocabulary words. One feature that these websites share is test mode, where users can quiz themselves and see their progress. Another feature includes practicing the vocabulary words in different games, such as 'Jewels of Wisdom' or 'Stellar Speller' on *Cram*, 'Match' or 'Gravity' on *Quizlet*, and 'Crossword' and 'Hungry Bug' on *StudyStack*.

Table 1.   Student-teachers' demographics

Participant	Gender	Nationality/ First Language	Age	Years of Teaching Experience	Grade Level
A	Female	Pakistan/Urdu	30-34	10+	College - University
B	Female	United Kingdom/ English	25-29	3-5	College - University
C	Female	Bahrain/Arabic	20-24	1-2	Intermediate
D	Female	Bahrain/Arabic	20-24	1-2	Primary - Elementary
E	Male	Indonesia/Bahasa Indonesia	20-24	3-5	College - University

For additional features, users can pay a fee to upgrade their membership. These features include removing any advertisements and adding an unlimited number of folders to organise a user's flashcards. *Cram, Quizlet,* and *StudyStack* also have corresponding Smartphone apps, which is an important element in maintaining flexible access to flashcards. This aligns with Nation's (2011) belief that "the best [computer programmes] are those which can be used on a cell phone or an iPod so that the learner has flexibility in choosing when to do the learning" (p. 53).

Hubbard's (2011) methodological framework for evaluating websites was selected to construct the questions in the survey and the semi-structured focus group discussion. As part of the coding process for the Likert-scale items in the survey, the six responses were grouped into Agree and Disagree categories. An interpretative qualitative approach was utilised for the analysis of the data retrieved from the focus group discussion and open-ended questions from the survey. Coding of the data, as recommended by Miles and Huberman (1994), included tallying the rate of recurrence, observing any patterns, and sorting the data into categories.

3.   Discussion

3.1.   What are student-teachers' beliefs concerning the usability of *Cram, Quizlet,* and *StudyStack*?

Usability, or the website's ability to "effectively and efficiently" fulfill users' needs (Lim & Lee, 2007, p. 68), can be determined from two perspectives: technical and pedagogical. This is because evaluating websites from only one perspective, or their technical usability, is not sufficient if they will be used for learning (Lim & Lee, 2007). As Lim and Lee (2007, p. 75) highlight, both usabilities are "intertwined" given that technical usability does not necessarily contribute to the websites' effectiveness on learners. Accordingly, the beliefs of student-teachers regarding both technical and pedagogical usabilities will be discussed.

3.1.1.   Technical usability

Computer and internet access were the issues that were first highlighted by the student-teachers (Alnajjar & Brick, 2017). However, student-teachers mentioned that the problem of accessibility could be resolved if their learners had access to these websites and apps on their phones, as emphasised in the extract below (Focus Group Discussion, 26 November 2015).

> **Participant A:** "…If you want to use the applications, it's easier for the students to just pull out their devices and use that because they're in our hands… Very few people open their laptops because all the classes in Pakistan don't have computers. It's just the Language Lab. Almost every student has an iPhone. Android is a must. So, it's easier to ask [the students] to bring out their phones and use the apps. Like one of the websites said, 'Vocabulary on the go'. The advertising is really true. You can *learn* and *create* flashcards on the go".

> **Participant B:** "Then, it will be a resource for everybody in the class to use whenever they want".

In addition, survey responses revealed that student-teachers favoured *Quizlet* more than *Cram* and *StudyStack*. *StudyStack*'s design was unanimously disliked, as they mentioned that it was "outdated", "old-fashioned", "crowded", and had a lot of information "jammed into a little space" (Alnajjar & Brick, 2017).

3.1.2. Pedagogical usability

All student-teachers held positive attitudes towards digital flashcards, as they saw the potential of the CAVL tool, particularly *Quizlet*, in creating motivated English language learners and prompting those learners to practice the newly acquired vocabulary words. This was compatible with Chien's (2015) findings, where he reached the conclusion that this CAVL tool motivated the English language learners in his study to learn more vocabulary. The participants in his study, who were first-year university students taking English classes, also preferred using *Quizlet* more than the other two websites.

In addition to learners' motivation, student-teachers agreed that the website's user-friendliness played a role in its usability. For instance, one reason why *Quizlet* was preferred to the other two websites was because the student-teachers felt that it was easier to use, gave teachers more information about their learners' progress, and is teacher- and learner-centred.

3.2. What variables shape student-teachers' beliefs?

The first variable was the 'wow' factor (Murray & Barnes, 1998), as some of the student-teachers' positive or negative reactions were based on initial exposure. The second variable was learners' age, where they felt that the availability of games on the websites could be of interest to young learners. This exemplifies that learners' age influences many pedagogical decisions, in addition to materials selection, in the classroom. The third variable was the quality of the graphics on the websites. Student-teachers believe that their learners may not engage in websites with low-quality graphics. The fourth variable was student-teachers' previous experience with using CAVL tools. This is because they had used one of these websites in their learning on the MA course and found the experience both useful and successful.

3.3. Will student-teachers incorporate digital flashcards in their classroom practice?

Student-teachers can have a unique standpoint when evaluating CAVL tools, as they can reflect on their learners' experience, as well as their own. They were not against the use of digital flashcards as a blended learning tool in their teaching, but were hesitant towards training learners. Consequently, it would be difficult to conclusively determine whether they will incorporate this tool in their classrooms. Nonetheless, student-teachers mentioned that their learners can access digital flashcards outside the classroom, which will subsequently minimise classroom time spent on familiarising learners with the tool.

To make the process of incorporating digital flashcards in the English classroom easier, we suggest following Hubbard's (2004) framework:

- having student-teachers experience the tool themselves to understand their learners' perspectives;

- giving learners training to help them become autonomous and understand the purpose of using the CAVL tool for their learning goals;

- using a 'cyclical approach' to training, where training is cumulative and continuous;

- using 'collaborative debriefings', where learners discuss their experience with each other; and

- teaching learners 'general exploitation strategies' of the CAVL tool to increase their control of it and to help them utilise these acquired strategies with other tools.

4.   Conclusions

Five student-teachers participated in this study and explored the usability of *Cram, Quizlet,* and *StudyStack*. There was a consensus amongst them regarding their preferred website, which was *Quizlet*. Furthermore, they felt that the additional affordances of digital flashcards, as opposed to physical flashcards, could be advantageous to English language learners when implementing a blended learning approach to teaching vocabulary. However, due to the student-teachers' unease around training learners in the use of digital flashcards, they appeared to be somewhat reluctant to integrate them into their classroom, so a future study could investigate adoption rates and practice with flashcards vis-à-vis teachers' positive beliefs towards them. Moreover, the lack of agreement amongst them with regards to the most effective way of blending a CAVL tool in their English language classrooms highlights the need for more research in this area.

References

Alnajjar, M., & Brick, B. (2017). Utilizing computer-assisted vocabulary learning tools in English language teaching: examining in-service teachers' beliefs of the usability of digital flashcards. *International Journal of Computer-Assisted Language Learning and Teaching, 7*(1), 1-18. https://doi.org/10.4018/IJCALLT.2017010101

Chien, C. (2015). Analysis the effectiveness of three online vocabulary flashcard websites on L2 learners level of lexical knowledge. *English Language Teaching, 8*(5), 111-121. https://doi.org/10.5539/elt.v8n5p111

Cram. (2015). *Cram.* http://www.cram.com

Dörnyei, Z. (2007). *Research methods in applied linguistics.* Oxford University Press.

Hubbard, P. (2004). Learner training for effective use of CALL. In S. Fotos & C. Browne (Eds), *New perspectives on CALL for second language classrooms* (pp. 45-68). Lawrence Erblaum.

Hubbard, P. (2011). Evaluation of courseware and websites. In L. Ducate & N. Arnold (Eds), *Present and future perspectives of CALL: from theory and research to new directions in foreign language teaching* (2nd ed., pp. 407-440). CALICO.

Lim, C., & Lee, S. (2007). Pedagogical usability checklist for ESL/EFL eLearning websites. *Journal of Convergence Information Technology, 2*(3), 67-76.

Miles, M., & Huberman, A. (1994). *Qualitative data analysis* (2nd ed.). SAGE Publications.

Murray, L., & Barnes, A. (1998). Beyond the 'Wow' factor: evaluating multimedia language learning software from a pedagogical viewpoint. *System, 26*, 249-259. https://doi.org/10.1016/S0346-251X(98)00008-6

Nakata, T. (2011). Computer-assisted second language vocabulary learning in a paired-associate paradigm: a critical investigation of flashcard software. *Computer Assisted Language Learning, 24*(1), 17-38. https://doi.org/10.1080/09588221.2010.520675

Nation, I. S. P. (2011). My ideal vocabulary teaching course. In J. Macalister & I. S. P. Nation (Eds), *Case studies in language curriculum design: concepts and approaches in action around the world* (pp. 49-62). Routledge.

Nation, I. S. P. (2013). *Learning vocabulary in another language* (2nd ed.). Cambridge University Press. https://doi.org/10.1017/CBO9781139858656

Quizlet. (2015). *Quizlet.* https://quizlet.com

Schmitt, N. (2008). Review article: instructed second language vocabulary learning. *Language Teaching Research, 12*(3), 329-363. https://doi.org/10.1177/1362168808089921

StudyStack. (2015). *StudyStack.* http://www.studystack.com

Author index